Guiding Students into Information Literacy

Strategies for Teachers and Teacher-Librarians

Chris Carlson
Ellen Brosnahan

THE SCARECROW PRESS, INC.
Lanham, Maryland • Toronto • Plymouth, UK
2009

SCARECROW PRESS, INC.

Published in the United States of America
by Scarecrow Press, Inc.
A wholly owned subsidary of The Rowman & Littlefield Publishing Group, Inc.
4501 Forbes Boulevard, Suite 200, Lanham, Maryland 20706
www.scarecrowpress.com

Estover Road
Plymouth PL6 7PY
United Kingdom

British Library Cataloguing in Publication Information Available

Library of Congress Cataloging-in-Publication Data

Carlson, Chris, 1948–
  Guiding students into information literacy : Strategies for teachers and teacher-librarians / Chris Carlson,
Ellen Brosnahan.
      p. cm.
  Includes bibliographical references and index.
  ISBN-13: 978-0-8108-5974-6 (pbk. : alk. paper)
  ISBN-10: 0-8108-5974-2 (pbk. : alk. paper)
  ISBN-13: 978-0-8108-6355-2 (ebook)
  ISBN-10: 0-8108-6355-3 (ebook)
  1. Information literacy–Study and teaching (Middle school)–United States. 2. Research–
Methodology–Study and teaching (Middle school)–United States. 3. Report writing–Study and
teaching (Middle school)–United States. 4. Library orientation for middle school children–
United States. 5. School librarian participation in curriculum planning. I. Brosnahan, Ellen, 1949–
II. Title.
  ZA3075.C3557 2009
  028.7071073–dc22   2008029191

∞™ The paper used in this publication meets the minimum requirements of
American National Standard for Information Sciences—Permanence of Paper
for Printed Library Materials, ANSI/NISO Z39.48-1992.
Manufactured in the United States of America.

Contents

List of Figures

Introduction

Grading These Research Papers Is Putting Me to Sleep

"All right, students! Here we go! Today is the day we'll begin viewing the PowerPoint presentations you've been working on for the past two weeks. I am sure we'll all learn about the contributions that our early presidents made toward developing our nation. Who'd like to go first?"

Nervously, the eighth graders glanced around, none of them wanting to be the first up. Finally, after a long silence, Jack, a confident and outgoing young man, waved his arm. "I'll go first, Mr. Teckie," he said as he strode to the front of the room.

Mr. Teckie settled in. Jack was one of his best students, and he was expecting an interesting, in-depth presentation. Jack began, and dancing letters paraded across the screen announcing, "George Washington was born in ____. He died in ____." Some basic facts about our first president, arranged in attractive bullets, followed, and a glitzy-looking "The End" culminated the presentation. Jack smiled, then returned to his seat.

Meanwhile, Mr. Teckie groaned inside. Where was the in-depth analysis of a president's contribution? Where were the specific strengths and weaknesses of the president? Where, oh, where were any of Jack's ideas or opinions on George Washington?

Next up was Tiffani, followed by Ashley, followed by Tyrone. Each PowerPoint featured cool fonts, letters that zipped in and out of the screen. But, alas! Only bare bones information that could have been found in any basic encyclopedia entry appeared while students read the facts aloud to their classmates. *This is not what I had in mind*, thought Mr. Teckie, as his eyes, and those of his students, seemed to glaze over in boredom.

At lunchtime, Mr. Teckie slumped into the faculty room where he saw his colleague, Miss Frazzle, sipping a cup of coffee behind a pile of essays.

"How were your PowerPoints today, Joe? The students sure seemed excited about doing all of that work in the computer lab."

"Well," he replied, "I wanted the students to really sink their teeth into learning about their topic, to be able to determine what made each president unique, but seems like they focused only on fancy letters and fonts, with no substance. I don't get it!"

Miss Frazzle pointed to the pile of papers in front of her and sighed. "I know what you mean. Yesterday I collected one hundred twenty-five research papers on France from my seventh graders, and I began grading them last night." She picked up a paper dressed in a shiny plastic cover from the top of the stack. "I keep thinking, 'Maybe this one will be the fresh, informative project I had hoped for when I assigned the research project.'" She began to read aloud, "'I did my report on France.' See what I mean?" Miss Frazzle's eyes skimmed the paper. Following that not-so-compelling lead were the same snippets of information that Miss Frazzle found in the previous papers she had read, and the language and sentence structure was suspiciously similar to that found in the *World Book Encyclopedia*, volume F. She sighed and rolled her eyes heavenward. "Where have I gone wrong?" she wondered. "Why can't my students research well and write an interesting paper?"

Just then, the faculty lounge door opened and Mrs. Bookly, the school's teacher-librarian, entered to get a cup of coffee. "Gee, Marsha, you look tired. And Joe, you look kind of down in the dumps, too. What's the matter?" she inquired.

"We were just commiserating," Mr. Teckie said. "We both assigned research projects to our students. My classes did PowerPoint presentations on early presidents, and they just weren't what I had hoped they'd be."

"Yes, and I just hoped these research papers would be better. But they aren't," sighed Miss Frazzle.

Mrs. Bookly sat down and picked up a paper from the pile. "Oh, it was your class that was looking for information on France! I wondered why my shelves were being cleaned out! I was so frustrated that I couldn't help them all."

"Yes, it was my assignment. Lots of students told me that all the information on France was gone from the library media center when they went in during study hall time to check out a book."

"I didn't really know what they needed to learn about France either," Miss Bookly continued. "I suggested some other sources where they could find information, but some of the students didn't seem to know how to use online sources very well."

"I agree that they don't seem to have good researching skills, but I don't know what I can do. I can't help everyone at once, no matter how hard I try." With this statement Miss Frazzle put her head in her hands.

"And, Joe," Mrs. Bookly continued, "I didn't know your students were researching, either."

"Well, I told them to go online to find stuff, and then we worked in the computer lab for a few days. But all they got were some basic facts."

"Marsha, Joe, if I had known what you needed ahead of time . . ."

"Really? I guess I never considered checking with you," Miss Frazzle admitted.

"Neither did I," said Mr. Teckie.

Now it was Mrs. Bookly's turn to sigh. "So few teachers do. Then all of their students want the same materials at the same time. And to complicate matters, many students don't know how to search for information either. I run around the library media center trying to help everyone at once, but I don't feel like I am really helping anyone, especially in regards to helping them find what they need for the assignment or how to search effectively."

"Wow, sounds like we are all frustrated and concerned that the students aren't learning as much as they could," commented Mr. Teckie.

"That's for sure. Say, let's put our heads together next time. Why don't we sit down and plan before you give the assignment. We can consider what outcomes you have in mind for students. I could even do some lessons on finding information, evaluating sources . . ."

"That'd be great! Let's do it! I wish we had talked with you about this before I assigned this report," Miss Frazzle said ruefully.

"Live and learn," was the reply.

Most classroom teachers have student research horror stories. It seems that no matter how extensively we plan, how thoroughly we explain, or how diligently we keep tabs on our students, there are disasters, disappointments, and foul-ups lurking around every corner. Teacher-librarians have their frustrations, too. They are often unable to help students because the classroom teachers who assign research projects fail to keep them informed about what the students will need to do to complete the assignment. These same teachers don't convey the kind of information they expect students to find in order to complete the assignment. Communication between classroom teachers and teacher-librarians is the key to research success and must occur before a project begins, while the project is underway, and also after the project has been completed. Teachers and teacher-librarians who work together as a team of educators know that students will reap the rewards that come from this collaboration and probably will find the process of doing research an enjoyable experience and much easier as well.

Do any of these discouraging comments from students sound familiar to you?

"Why do we have to do this?"

"But I'm not a good researcher."

"The library has no stuff on my topic."

"We did a research report last year."

In this book we will tackle some of these familiar refrains and maybe even a few you haven't encountered (yet). Each can be avoided or minimized by careful planning and by using proven strategies for maximizing the research experience for your students. Using the comments we have heard from actual students, each chapter in this book will look at a different aspect of a research project. This book will discuss ways in which teachers can use student complaints and concerns to turn the "whine" into vintage research experiences that are both instructional and meaningful. With careful, reasoned planning and management strategies, students can have a worthwhile research experience, and teachers will find that assessing the students' work can be an enjoyable task.

For many years we have worked with eighth-grade students on an I-search project. An I-search is an inquiry-based project that allows students to choose topics of interest to them. Each student's research is guided by questions that the student has about his topic that he wishes to answer through careful research. The student researcher logs his actions, questions, and thoughts during the search process. Because each student has a different set of questions that he is hoping to answer, the results of the research differ from student to student even though the topic could be the same. After the student is satisfied by his quest for answers and has learned essential things about the topic he has chosen, the student organizes his findings and reports on what he has found. In our I-search project the final report is a paper written in the first person. In it the author describes why he selected the topic, what questions guided the search, what he discovered during the search process, and what surprises or problems he encountered during the activity. Because writers are encouraged to include their own voice in the writing, I-search papers avoid the dry, third-person tone of the traditional research paper.

After the I-search papers are collected, assessed, and returned to the students, we, the classroom teacher and the teacher-librarian, meet to consider the successes and failures of the project and whether the activity has been valuable for the students. Because we feel that research needs to be meaningful, we are constantly looking for ways to improve the I-search project. Our assessments at the completion of the I-search activity each year have led us to develop many of the tools and strategies we cover in this book. Drawing on our experiences over years of teaching information literacy skills and managing research projects, we suggest ways to guide students from choosing an appropriate topic to handing in the paper. We want to offer other teachers the hope that student research experiences can be both instructive to students and also a worthwhile undertaking for the teacher. Students can understand the value of research and learn skills that will serve them whenever they are faced with an information need. Teachers who look critically at their research assignments and provide students with the tools to be successful are taking the first steps to creating experiences that will fill them with wonder at their students' knowledge and creativity. Although much of this book is based on our experience with the I-search paper, the procedures are easily transferable to *any* kind of research students do. No matter what the format the end assessment takes, we all want our students to become better researchers and critical thinkers.

In the next few chapters we use student comments as the springboard for discussing ways that teachers and teacher-librarians can manage the entire research experience and make it valuable for everyone involved.

"Why do we have to do this?" Middle and high school students love to challenge the relevance of school assignments, and they often ask this. This is, however, an excellent question, and one that every teacher should ask before time and effort are devoted to any assignment. In our first chapter, we discuss how teachers need to consider the lifelong learning benefits of a research project to a student. We challenge teachers to take a deeper look at an old favorite assignment and determine the content and learner outcomes it fosters as well as the complex thinking strategies it requires. We suggest ways to assess whether these outcomes are attained. To give students a richer and more valuable experience, we feel that it is important to focus on what the process is supposed to teach the students. It is important to also determine whether a full-blown research project is what you want or if a different kind of assignment will suffice. When you decide ahead of time if your desired outcome is to teach a concept, the research process, information literacy skills, or a combination of all of these, the strategies and activities you use will be much more focused.

"There's no stuff in this library on my topic" is a familiar refrain. This chapter demonstrates how planning ahead with teacher-librarians will ensure that students are able to successfully complete the assignment while using the resources of the library media center (LMC) and the trained professional who runs it. Teachers need to understand the unique and important role that the teacher-librarian serves in the school community. We believe that having a good working relationship with your teacher-librarian can pay dividends both in the planning stage and during the course of the project.

The next chapter, "Why can't I research UFOs?" discusses how teachers can decide on appropriate and manageable topics for their students. One of our students took a very humanitarian approach to choosing a topic and said, "My topic is on what we can do to solve all the world's problems." Admirable, yes. Doable? Not quite! Another student stated, "My mother doesn't want me to research satanic cults." Who could blame her? We discuss how to get students focused in on a topic that is acceptable and how to get parents involved without having them do the work for the student.

Students often dread the research or term paper because it means they will have to work. "This sounds hard" will deal with ways to get students focused on the process by modeling assignments done by previous classes. This chapter also deals with how students' work can be guided by determining what will be assessed before the assignment is given. Not only do we provide suggestions on how to construct these assessment tools, we also give numerous examples of assessment tools that have worked successfully for us.

After the assignment is given, students realize that they need to find information on a topic, but many have no idea what they are searching for or even what form the final project will take. "I don't know where to start" is a familiar comment. Some students begin by checking out a big pile of books, intending to skim them all. Though this approach might seem industrious, it may not be the most efficient use of time. We have found that having students read one entire nonfiction book from cover to cover rather than hopping from one source to another is the best way to begin a project. Not only does this help students gain a better understanding of their topic, this activity is often the jump start that students need to get them engaged in a topic and gives direction to their ensuing research.

Perhaps the biggest hassle of student research is time management. In "I'm not a good researcher," we deal with the methods we have used to make sure students use their research time wisely. Although our students may never have actually voiced this idea, we have read it in their eyes: "Going to the LMC? Cool! I get to talk to my friends and just pretend to look busy." In order to promote actual "research gathering" rather than "friendly socializing," we suggest that schools adopt a research model that systematically teaches information literacy skills and can be called upon whenever the student is faced with an information need. Unlike other books on student research, we do not intend to detail the steps in teaching information skills. There are numerous books on the market that do an excellent job of this, and we include many of them in the reading lists that are found at the end of each chapter. Instead, we talk about how we have been able to effectively use these proven research models so that students can develop important information literacy skills. We also discuss the value of developing and using research organizers that help the student follow the research model you, the teacher, have selected. No longer accepting excuses such as "I'm not a good researcher," teachers can use our proven methods for keeping students on task.

"Four weeks until the due date? Awesome! That means I can relax for four weeks and get it all done the night before." While students may not actually say these words, it does seem to be their modus operandi at times. Even the most well intentioned among us have been guilty of procrastination or underestimating the time necessary to complete a project. By using daily exit slips and thinking logs to prevent procrastination, we have kept those quiet, busy-looking kids from slipping beneath the teacher radar. We provide examples of these tools with suggestions on making them work for your assignment. Students will no longer be able to put off work, hoping to put everything together the night before it's due.

During the research process, little problems can become big ones. Some simple organizational strategies can prevent those chilling words, "Uh, oh! I lost all my notecards" or "Bibliography? I don't know the title of the book I used, but I remember it was heavy." And, though students are often told to take notes and put things in their own words, few understand how to do this. Although we advocate that note-taking skills be taught, modeled, and practiced, rather than concentrating on how to teach these skills, we instead discuss ways to get students' thoughts and reactions into their notes. "Where's that green book I used yesterday?" tackles some of the organizational problems that seem to elude student researchers. We also provide examples of forms that allow students to organize their notes and remember the information sources they have used.

Once the research time is over, it is time to for the student to reveal the results of her research. This book concentrates on an assignment that resulted in a written I-search paper. It is amazing how some students think that a laser printer, spell check, and a shiny plastic cover are all they need to make their paper stand out. We are not bamboozled by the fancy trappings but are more interested in content. After spending weeks of valuable class time on this project, we are concerned about what the students have actually learned. Have they grown in their content knowledge? Have they learned new and effective research techniques? Have they written a clear and engaging piece? This next chapter provides a proven method for getting students to organize their notes into a cohesive paper. It covers the advantages of having the students write in the first person as a way to make the paper more interesting for the reader and also gives students an opportunity to voice their own opinions and thoughts. Although many students may say "It's not supposed to be interesting—it's a report," the teachers who need to read through a class full of papers will understand how important it is to make sure the papers do not just regurgitate facts, imitating the lifeless entries in an encyclopedia. This chapter also includes various evaluation tools that can be used with a class before the final paper is submitted, aiding students in preparing a final draft that is interesting to read, rich in content, and relatively free of grammatical errors.

One of the biggest problems teachers encounter is how to deal with plagiarism. Internet sites that sell research papers are plentiful. Students sometimes do not understand the importance of putting thoughts and information in their own words. In "I can copy it off the Internet," we discuss the issue of plagiarism, sharing our methods for how we combat it and suggesting ways to spot plagiarism.

"Not another written report!" How many times do teachers hear this common complaint? Reports or research papers seem to flash "boring" in front of the eyes of students who are constantly bombarded by flashy websites and multimedia. This chapter provides some alternatives to the traditional research paper and gives several suggestions for extending student research into other creative projects.

The final chapter, "When will I ever use this stuff?" provides information on current research that emphasizes the importance of teaching students those important information literacy skills that they will gain by a structured and well-thought-out research assignment.

Each chapter zeroes in on issues that stand in the way of success. To help those who want to improve student research, we provide numerous tools we have used to support the process. We list websites and books that readers can reference for additional information and ideas on the content provided in each chapter. And, to further convince teachers that it is possible for students to compose an interesting, fact-filled research paper, we have provided several examples of actual student work in the appendixes. We believe that students can write interesting research reports, they can extend research into other types of assignments, and their efforts will bring them satisfaction. This book hopes to underscore the worthiness of taking the time to teach research skills and fashion an assignment that will bring out the best in each student, whether it be a written report, a PowerPoint presentation, or a podcast. One thing we have found is that after completing our I-search assignment, students are able to transfer the management, communication, and information literacy skills they have gained because of this experience to any other type of research project.

Written in the first person, like the I-search paper we prefer to use with our eighth-grade students, this book will detail the strategies we have developed to help our students learn how to research, how to write, and, perhaps, how to enjoy the entire research process. And it is our hope that after using the techniques in this book, any teacher who finds herself sitting at the kitchen table or at a desk reading her students' research reports will reach eagerly for the next informative and compelling one in the pile.

1

Why Do We Have to Do This?

"Why do we have to do this?"

"What's the point?"

Although these statements might seem like just so much teenage complaining, these are questions that every teacher should ask before embarking on a research project. With only about 176 instructional days per year on the calendar, school days are packed! Research takes time, a most precious commodity. Do you really want to use this valuable time on meaningless, fluffy projects or on assignments that fail to teach important skills, strategies, or concepts? It is important to take a critical look at what we do in our classrooms, especially those favorite projects.

Many well-intentioned teachers have projects that seem to be research related. On closer scrutiny, however, the learning opportunities for students are rather shallow. Have you experienced that sinking feeling that things haven't gone as you expected? Even though those research papers that have been slipped into shiny plastic covers may look promising, oftentimes they are filled with inaccurate or skimpy information that begs the question, "What have we been doing all this time?"

And bad research activities don't always have to take the form of a written piece. Have you seen student-created posters with glittery letters and cool graphics but little or no useful information? Have students sometimes spent loads of classroom time and energy planning a skit, complete with flashy costumes and props but devoid of substance? Teachers must look beyond the cute covers, the glitzy posters, and the fun skits to see if the hours devoted to researching, writing, and presenting these activities provided valuable learning opportunities for the students.

So, where can you begin? First, I suggest that you concentrate on the results. There is no more important question to ponder when planning than "What knowledge will students acquire during this assignment? How will the project extend their understanding and skill set?"

CONTENT AND LEARNING OUTCOMES

Consider the lifelong learning benefits that the student will gain by engaging in the project. Lifelong learning benefits include the abilities to engage in complex thinking, to process information, to communicate effectively, and to work collaboratively with others. These qualities of lifelong learning require that students develop good personal habits that will stretch their minds. In designing a research project for my eighth-grade language arts students, I began by considering these lifelong learning benefits. I wanted students to become familiar with the variety of print and electronic sources available to them in the school library and to be able to process information from a variety of sources. It was also vital that they develop the skills necessary to take notes, organize information, and write a clear and detailed paper using the information they found. I wanted them to communicate effectively by expressing ideas and opinions clearly. During the course of the project, I wanted the students to develop some beneficial habits of mind, including the ability to follow a reasoned plan, to be open-minded, and to persevere through any difficulties to a successful completion. Once I identified these learning outcomes, they became the centerpiece for the project I was planning.

Another crucial thing to consider in planning a research unit is deciding what topics should be chosen for research. The first time I assigned a research project, I allowed the students to have unlimited choices on topics, telling myself that students should be able to choose whatever topic interested them. Some students zeroed in on concerns that they had, such as improving the environment. Others looked at the project as an opportunity to learn more about a topic in which they had an interest, such as plate tectonics. But others took a less lofty route. Some students wanted to learn about the Bermuda Triangle. Others wished to focus on their favorite rock group or athlete. Still other students had difficulty determining exactly what they wanted to learn about and had trouble selecting any topic at all. After reading some dismal papers, I looked more closely at content outcomes. Although it was important that students be able to access and use information and create a well-written piece, I felt that it would be an added bonus if students actually learned some valuable information along the way. While spending a month or so reading about Britney Spears may be loads of fun, can we really devote valuable instructional time to this endeavor?

To improve my project, I chose to have the students focus their research on an issue that had an impact on today's world by challenging them to consider the following questions with regard to their topic: "How did we get to where we are today? How has our past shaped our present? How will we cope? How should we manage the challenges of life that face our society today? What are the best ways to deal with these issues?" This challenged them to dig deeply into a concern or issue and form an opinion about it. As a result, students would not only learn how to research and write effectively, they also would gain a better understanding of the complex issues that grab the newspaper headlines or are flashed across television news channels every day.

Although my "concerns" project was chosen for the language arts classroom, assigning research projects in the disciplines of social studies, science, mathematics, and the arts provides myriad opportunities for meeting specific content outcomes while developing students' research skills. What better way for students to understand the concepts and molecular structure of chemical elements than to have them create a threefold brochure on a particular element for a science class? Analyzing an artist's paintings will challenge students to learn about artistic movements and better understand what inspired an artist to create as he did. These are just two ideas that can be used by teachers in disciplines other than language arts. By building a research project around an instructional concept that teachers want their students to understand or by allowing students to direct their own learning by searching out information, teachers can use quick research projects as an important instructional tool.

Tying the research project to district or national standards will make doing the project worthwhile and give the project purpose. Recently, a lot of work has been done by dedicated education professionals who have developed learning standards in many of the disciplines. Most states have education standards that are easily accessible either on the Web or available in your school library or district curriculum office.

In addition to state standards, lots of individual school districts have their own learning standards based on those of the state. Sometimes these districts will also provide samples of possible assignments or reproducible worksheets that are meant to aid teachers in developing units or teaching essential information literacy skills. Figure 1.1 is an example of a standard developed by a school district for their language arts curriculum. This example addresses the standard that deals with how students will access and use information.

In addition to state or district learning standards for language arts, several organizations have also developed standards related to writing and information literacy. It is often a good idea to assure yourself that your project falls in line with standards developed by any of these organizations.

Websites developed by professional organizations also allow visitors to purchase numerous books based on the standards developed by their members. Many of these publications provide handy worksheets or examples of research projects that can be adapted to meet the needs of any teacher who is interested in developing his or her own project based on these learning standards.

If you or your school library does not have a copy of these standards, consult the following websites to find standards by state or subject area: http://edstandards.org/Standards.html or http://www.middleschool.net/standads/standrd.htm. Another website that contains articles and tools for those who want to develop standards is http://www.mcrel.org/standards-benchmarks.

After determining the content and the learner outcomes, it is important to examine whether the project will foster complex thinking processes. Often students are asked only to find information and restate it. With a little more planning, students can do more with the information they gather. Instead of simply reporting on a Civil War general (biographical stuff), why not evaluate his impact on the outcome of the war? What about ranking? Forming an opinion? Persuading an audience to embrace a particular point of view? All of these suggestions enrich the research experience and foster complex thinking skills.

The American Association of School Librarians (http://www.ala.org/aasl) and the National Council of Teachers of English (http://www.ncte.org) are two such well-respected organizations. Visiting their websites will lead you to copies of the standards they have developed. In addition, the following websites will lead you to standards for the following content areas: Mathematics (http://www.nctm.org); Science (http://www.nsta.org/standards); Geography (http://www.ncge.org/publications/tutorial/standards/); History (http://www.sscnet.ucla.edu/nchs/standards).

Standard 8 – Accessing and Using Information
    The student conducts research on issues and interest by generating ideas and questions and by posing problems. The student gathers, evaluates, and synthesizes data from a variety of sources (e.g. print, non-print, artifacts, people) to communicate the discoveries in ways that suit their purpose and audience.

Indicator 1: The student initiates the research process

Grade 6	Grade 7	Grade 8
Identifies appropriate topics	Identifies appropriate topics	Identifies appropriate topics
Can narrow topic (chronologically and/or topically and/or geographically	Can narrow topic (chronologically and/or topically and/or geographically	Can narrow topic (chronologically and/or topically and/or geographically
Formulates questions related to topic	Formulates questions related to topic	Formulates questions related to topic
Identifies a variety of primary and secondary sources of information related to topic	Identifies a variety of primary and secondary sources of information related to topic	Identifies a variety of primary and secondary sources of information related to topic

Indicator 2: The student selects appropriate sources to be used in research and evaluates these sources

Grade 6	Grade 7	Grade 8
Develops a list of keywords	Develops a list of keywords	Develops a list of keywords
Locates a variety of accurate sources and narrows them to those that are best for the task at hand	Locates a variety of accurate sources and narrows them to those that are best for the task at hand	Locates a variety of accurate sources and narrows them to those that are best for the task at hand
Uses appropriate strategies to find information • Refines search using Boolean operators • Uses call numbers to locate books on shelf • Uses indexes, tables of contents, etc. to locate information within each source	Uses appropriate strategies to find information • Refines search using Boolean operators • Uses call numbers to locate books on shelf • Uses indexes, tables of contents, etc. to locate information within each source	Uses appropriate strategies to find information • Refines search using Boolean operators • Uses call numbers to locate books on shelf • Uses indexes, tables of contents, etc. to locate information within each source
	Separates facts from opinions	Separates facts from opinion
		Determines the accuracy, relevance, timeliness and comprehensiveness of the information found
		Recognizes point of view and bias

Indicator 3: The student manages the information

Grade 6	Grade 7	Grade 8
Records information in an appropriate note-taking format	Records information in an appropriate note-taking format	Records information in an appropriate note-taking format
Expands search or revises original questions as necessary	Expands search or revises original questions as necessary	Expands search or revises original questions as necessary
Organizes information in a practical, organized manner (e.g. sorts notecards, outlines, uses graphic organizer)	Organizes information in a practical, organized manner (e.g. sorts notecards, outlines, uses graphic organizer)	Organizes information in a practical, organized manner (e.g. sorts notecards, outlines, uses graphic organizer)
Analyzes information for accuracy and relevancy	Analyzes information for accuracy and relevancy	Analyzes information for accuracy and relevancy

Middle School Language Arts: Indicators of Learning   DRAFT   10/2/98

Uses a sufficient number of sources	Uses a sufficient number of sources	Uses a sufficient number of sources

Indicator 4: The student demonstrates understanding of the information by communicating it in an appropriate manner

Grade 6	Grade 7	Grade 8
Integrates new information into own knowledge	Integrates new information into own knowledge	Integrates new information into own knowledge
Presents information in a way that is understandable to others	Presents information in a way that is understandable to others	Presents information in a way that is understandable to others
Presents information in the appropriate form	Fulfills the defined need	Fulfills the defined need

Indicator 5: The student reflects on his/her growth

Grade 6	Grade 7	Grade 8
Evaluates the questions that drove the information need	Evaluates the questions that drove the information need	Evaluates the questions that drove the information need
Assesses whether enough sources were used and if these sources were appropriate for the task	Assesses whether enough sources were used and if these sources were appropriate for the task	Assesses whether enough sources were used and if these sources were appropriate for the task
Determines whether the information was communicated in ways that suit the purpose and audience	Determines whether the information was communicated in ways that suit the purpose and audience	Determines whether the information was communicated in ways that suit the purpose and audience

Fig. 1.1.   An example of a standard developed by a school district for their language arts curriculum.

PROCESS VS. PRODUCT

Classroom teachers often approach the teacher-librarian for suggestions on projects that involve using the school library (LMC) for research. In discussing what they might do, one of the first questions the teacher-librarian should ask is "What are you mainly interested in—the process or the product?" In other words, is the teacher interested in having the students learn how to research? What information sources available in the school library does the teacher want students to use? Is there enough time for students to learn the differ-ences and strengths of a particular information source? Does the classroom teacher have the time to allow the teacher-librarian to instruct students in important information literacy skills? Can she devote several days or weeks to the project? Or does the teacher want to assign a research assignment because he needs another grade in the book before the end of the grading period or because the curriculum requires that the students learn to write a persuasive essay?

If the important thing in a research assignment is the paper or product that the student crafts, it may not be necessary for students to learn to use all the information sources available in the school library at one time. There are many assignments that are simpler than a full-blown research project but that still require students to use some library resources. For example, if students need information to write a persuasive essay, one idea is to have the students use only periodicals for information. Not only will using magazines give students several perspectives on the issue and teach them about bias and opinion, the students will also have to learn how to use the periodical indexes, an important information literacy skill, during the course of their research. In a project about endangered species, students might be limited to finding information in a specialized encyclopedia on endangered animals and a science encyclopedia, such as Gale's Discovering Science, that is available online in the LMC. By using the information found in these specialized sources, students can speculate on what can be done to protect the animal they have chosen from becoming extinct. A biography unit could be limited to specific biographical sources, such as *Current Biography* and periodicals, rather than books or whole biographies about the person. In fact, limiting an assignment to one or two types of information sources is an excellent way for students to learn the ins and outs of a particular source. Creating such assignments—differing the type of source used with each but allowing students maximum exposure to each source—is an excellent way for them to really learn how to use many of the different information sources available in the school's library. Then, the next time students need to find information in this source, they will be familiar with the source's strengths and weaknesses, as well as knowing how to extract needed information from it.

If a classroom teacher chooses to have the teacher-librarian instruct students in the use of several information sources for the terms of the assignment, it is important that students have the time to actually use the source and become familiar with it before moving on to another source. If the students learn about the online catalog, Infotrac, and Newsbank all in one day, don't expect them to master any of them with proficiency. A more useful approach is to learn skills necessary for using a specific source, give students time to actually use it for research, and then move on to teaching about another source. Introducing too many sources at once can result in "information overload" and poorly learned skills, so that when students need to use one of the sources in the future, they might be left wondering how to use it again.

Sometimes it is not necessary that the students locate the best information sources themselves. Instead, they can practice finding the needed information in sources that have already been identified for them by the teacher or a teacher-librarian. In a "pathfinder" approach, students are given a list of sources chosen by the teacher-librarian and directed to find the information they need for their project by using the identified sources. Students need only go to these sources and relate the information found about their topic to the assignment. Figure 1.2 is an example of a pathfinder on the Great Depression for a project requiring students to write a letter to President Franklin D. Roosevelt, suggesting ideas for reforms that will help to alleviate hardships in their community.

Figure 1.3 is an example of a pathfinder developed by the teacher-librarian for a sixth-grade class that will make posters on important heroes in history. This pathfinder helps students identify keywords that will aid them in their search for information about a person.

In both of the previous examples, the pathfinder guides students to identified sources that will help them find essential information for their project. However, it is up to the student to extract the needed information from that source. Pathfinders can be a real aid to students in a research quest, especially for elementary students and novice researchers. Pathfinders also give novice researchers insight into how librarians find information and how seasoned researchers organize an information search.

> Teachers and teacher-librarians will find an excellent guide to constructing pathfinders at http://home.wsd.wednet.edu/pathfinders/path.htm and additional tools at http://eduscapes.com/earth/informational/path1.html. In addition, the Internet public library has examples of pathfinders for many subjects on their site, http://www.ipl.org/div/pf.

Techno-savvy instructors have created website/pathfinders and posted these pathfinders on their school's website so that they can be easily accessed by their students. A history teacher who wants her students to study the effects of war on soldiers who served in World War II might create a website/pathfinder that could include websites where students can find photos or interviews with WWII survivors, for example. Often these teacher-developed websites include active links to websites that have been checked out for the accuracy of content and for language that is appropriate for the age of their students. Developing your own "project website" is an excellent way for teachers to use the power of the Net without requiring that student researchers sift through hundreds of useless websites and search engines to find reliable information.

In recent years, Web quests have become popular. In a Web quest, students use only specially chosen Internet sites to gather the information needed to complete their project. Once again, although the sources are chosen by the classroom teacher, in a Web quest the students must extract the information from these sites, so they

THE GREAT DEPRESSION

The period in history when the United States economy had its biggest decline. It was characterized by decreasing business activity, falling prices, and high unemployment.

Where can you find information on the Great Depression in the learning resource center?

PRINT RESOURCES

Browse the books in reference and nonfiction with these call numbers:

973

973.9

973.91

Look in the SUBJECT index of the Haines catalog or Infotrac© for the following subjects:

Great Depression

U.S. – History, 1920–1929

U.S. – History, 1930–1939

Depressions – 1929 – United States

U.S. – Social life and customs – 1918–1945

GENERAL REFERENCE WORKS

R031	Encyclopedias
R973	Chronicle of America
R973	A History of US
973.9	20th Century America
973.91	UXL American Decades

ONLINE SOURCES

Online encyclopedias

American decades online

Student Resource Center (Infotrac, Discovering U.S. History)

Cobblestone online

INTERNET SITES

Information and links can be found at the following websites:

http://memory.loc.gov/ammem/fsowhome.html

http://www.amatecon.com/greatdepression.html

http://hoover.archives.gov/exhibits/Hooverstory/gallery06/gallery06.html

http://bergen.org/AAST/Projects/depression

http://www.42explore2.com/depresn.htm

http://www.historesearch.com/20sdep.html

http://webtech.kennesaw/adv/jcheck3/depression.htm

http://sos.state.mi.us/history/museum/explore/museums/hismus/
1900-75/depressn/labnew2/html

Fig. 1.2.   An example pathfinder on the Great Depression for a project requiring students to write a letter to President Franklin D. Roosevelt.

Biography Pathfinder

Biography is literature that attempts to record the life of a particular person

In searching for sources the following things are important and can lead you to books that contain information about a person:

1. The **person** himself.

   Look in the online catalog or indexes for the person's name (for example: JORDAN, Michael).

2. The person's **occupation**.

   Look in the online catalog under that occupation (for example: BASKETBALL PLAYERS) or look for a book that tells about persons who are in that occupation.

3. **Other people** with whom he had contact.

   Look for books about these people. Your person may be mentioned. (For example: you might find information about Al GORE in a book about Bill CLINTON.)

4. The **time period** in which your person lived.

   Look for history books (900s) that cover the period during which your person lived. (For example: You will find information about Al CAPONE in books about the 1920s.) Also, if your person is recently famous, you may find information in recent sources, like magazines, newspapers, or the internet.)

5. The **country** in which the person was born or where he lived.

   Look for books that cover the history of the country. (For example: You will find information about Saddam HUSSEIN in books that contain IRAQ.)

6. **Events** that occurred in which your person was involved.

   Look in indexes or the online catalog for that event. (For example: You will find information about Robert E. LEE in books about the CIVIL WAR.)

Fig. 1.3.   An example pathfinder for a sixth-grade class that will make posters on important heroes in history.

For more information on creating your own project website, check out the links at http://www.middleschool.net/curlink/interweb.htm or http://www.kn.att.com/wired/wired.html. Several browsers already offer teachers space for class websites. For more about tools and activities that use the technology of the 21st-century check http://21centuryconnections.com/learning.

do use complex thinking skills in order to process the information.

Another type of project that uses materials found in the school library but does not require that students learn how to locate the actual sources is for the teacher-librarian or subject-area teacher to collect all the print library materials available on the topic to be researched and to have them placed on a cart or shelf in the school library that is reserved for the class to use. Although it is not necessary for the students to search through the online catalog and the shelves in the school library to find these materials on their own, students must use these books, periodicals, media, and so forth to find the information needed to complete the assignment. This approach is particularly useful to "quick start" an assignment or to allow students instant access to library materials when the teacher-librarian knows that demand for terminals to use the online catalog will be heavy. Sometimes students in several classes may be searching for information or using the online catalog, thus causing backups at the computers, and when students cannot get access, they often become frustrated.

Some teachers, weary of reading written papers well into the night, have skipped the "product" part completely and just concentrated on the "process." One excellent idea for the type of assignment that concentrates on the process is to give students a topic and have them prepare their own pathfinders for that topic. An annotated bibliography also is an assignment that focuses on "process" more so than "product." By creating a pathfinder or an annotated bibliography, students learn about the diverse collection of materials available in the LMC without the additional time needed for taking notes and writing a paper. These types of assignments are less labor intensive for the teachers who will be assessing them but do provide classroom teachers and the teacher-librarian with a new approach to teaching important information skills. Asking the teacher-librarian to help assess these assignments can also be an excellent way for teachers and teacher-librarians to collaborate.

Information on constructing Web quests and examples of Web quests for many different subjects and grade levels can be found at http://webquest.sdsu.edu or http://www.webquest.org or http://bestwebquests.com.

The results of these pathfinders and/or bibliographies often help the teacher-librarian discover areas of weakness that may exist in the library collection.

When teachers come in to the library and tell the teacher-librarian, "My students are going to be using the library for the next three days, and I need you to show them how to find things in the school library," the teacher-librarian may suggest one of these simplified approaches that tie the project to learning research skills. Trying to teach kids how to use all the sources available—from the online catalog to the online reference sources to the periodical indexes to the Internet—in one day is like trying to get all of them to be perfect children. Impossible!

Teachers who are interested in having students learn the process must be willing to give the assignment the time and attention needed for the students to succeed. This means allowing enough time to learn how to research, to learn to distinguish between the sources that will be useful from those that are available, and to learn how to use each source effectively. These are important "information literacy skills" that students will use throughout their lives. Students deserve to be given the proper tools to ensure their success.

Those teachers who say "Well, they had to do a research paper last year, so they already know how to use all the stuff in the library" are somewhat cheating the kids. Online sources can change from year to year, the library can acquire new materials for students to use, and students new to the school will not be familiar with what is available. It never hurts students to have their information and retrieval skills reinforced, particularly at the junior high or middle school levels. We all know that often students forget over the summer much of what they have learned the prior year. And, just by chance, the guy who last year was too busy checking out the blonde in the front row may actually be interested in what the teacher-librarian has to say this year. Reinforcing information literacy skills when given the opportunity benefits students.

Most "traditional" research papers are a combination of process and product. Unfortunately, too often only the product is assessed. Teachers take for granted that students have used information literacy skills to produce the paper. However, I have found that giving both process and product equal value has resulted in better and more efficient research on the part of the students and a more interesting project for me to read and assess. I give some examples of things I have used to assess the process in a later chapter. It seems to me that if you want students to be information literate, making sure that students have the time to learn how to access and use information is an important part of teaching.

Once the focus of the project has been "nailed down," the teacher giving the assignment can plan activities that are related to getting good results and will be able to structure lesson plans that keep these outcomes in mind.

FURTHER READING

For more information on standards and outcomes, consult the following books:

Buzzeo, Toni. *Collaborating to Meet Standards: Teacher/Librarian Partnerships for 7–12.* Worthington, OH: Linworth, 2002.

Eisenberg, Michael, Carrie A. Lowe, and Kathleen Spitzer. *Information Literacy: Essential Skills for the Information Age.* 2nd ed. Westport, CT: Libraries Unlimited, 2004.

Information Power: Building Partnerships for Learning. Chicago: American Library Association, 1998.

Miller, Donna. *The Standards-Based Integrated Library.* 2nd ed. Worthington, OH: Linworth, 2004.

NCTE and IRA Joint Task Force on Assessment. *Standards for the English Language Arts.* Newark, DE: International Reading Association, 1996.

Pappas, Marjorie, and Ann E. Tepe. *Pathways to Knowledge.* Greenwood, CO: Libraries Unlimited and Teacher Ideas Press, 2002.

Thompson, Helen M., and Susan A. Henley. *Fostering Information Literacy: Connecting National Standards, Goals 2000 and the SCANS Report.* Englewood, CO: Libraries Unlimited and Teacher Ideas Press, 2000.

For more information on planning and producing websites, consult the following book:

McCorkle, Sandra K. *Web Pages for Your Classroom: The EASY Way!* Greenwood, CO: Libraries Unlimited, 2003.

2

There's No Stuff in This Library

Kids often spend valuable library research time wandering around the bookshelves looking lost or goofing off with other students. When one of these students is asked if he or she needs assistance, a common answer is, "There's no stuff on my topic in this library." And you know what? Sometimes they are correct!

Yes, sometimes the school library may not have any books on a topic. Imagine this scenario: A teacher wants every student in the class to do research on France. What does this mean for the school library that has only fifteen books about France? There could be fifty students clamoring to use the LMC's fifteen books on the country. Often, the first few students who make it to the LMC before the others in the class will rush to check out all the books on the topic, leaving no books for others to use.

Sometimes books are just not available because other classes are using them for an assignment. For example, if a sixth-grade social studies class is studying Greece, it probably would not be a good idea for seventh-grade language arts classes to begin a unit on myths because the sixth graders may be using most of the Greek mythology books.

Sometimes no books are available because of the topics that students have chosen to research. Often students choose topics that are obscure, and the school library just does not have an entire book on the topic. While there may be lots of books on art history, there are not whole books on the history of origami. And sometimes the library does not have books on a topic because there are none at the reading or understanding level of the student. Although there may be a book on the psychology of color, there certainly is not one at the level of most junior high or middle school students doing a science project.

What happens when one student is sitting with five books on his topic stacked in front of him but his friend is unable to find any on his topic? Kids lose confidence in libraries and librarians. Not only does this perplex the students, but it also frustrates even the best of teacher-librarians. For people who deal with information on a daily basis, it is discouraging to have to tell students that they are right when they say that there are no books on their topic available in the school library. No wonder so many students head directly to the Internet! Internet search engines will usually find a match with even the most obscure topics. Whether or not that information is useful is another matter. At least the person looking for information feels like he has something.

Just because the teacher-librarian cannot hand a student a book on his topic immediately does not mean that information on the student's topic is not available in reference sources that can't be checked out. It doesn't mean that the teacher-librarian can't borrow materials from other libraries and have them available for the student in a day or two. Unfortunately, kids have gotten used to getting things quickly and on demand, and that means they don't want to have to wait for materials or work hard to dig for the information.

Why doesn't the school library have something for everyone? Often the answer to that question has more to do with library budgets and school curriculum than with the topic a child has chosen to research. Teacher-librarians who are responsible for purchasing the materials for the school library would love to be able to buy everything that is published, but most school budgets don't allow for unlimited purchases. So, choices need to be made. Library book purchases are usually based on the school curriculum. If the teacher-librarian knows that the Civil War is studied in eighth-grade history but American Indians are not, any new titles on the Civil War become possible purchases, whereas the newest book on American Indians is optional and will be purchased only if enough money is available. Another thing that teacher-librarians take into consideration when choosing books for purchase is the age and reading level of the students at the school. Teacher-librarians want to be sure that the students are able to read and understand the material in the books they add to the collection in the school library. Teacher-librarians are aware that books that do not match up with students' ability levels will languish on the shelves. Some books, although scholarly, are either too difficult to understand or too intimidating for middle or junior high students or even some high schoolers. A lot of books that will have limited use are passed up in favor of those that will show their value because they will appeal to students and cover topics that are of interest to students in the school. Sometimes the most used books are those that look "elementary" because they are filled with pictures. Often, these elementary-looking books are chosen because they present quick information and are easily understood. Teacher-librarians know that students in high school, and even adults, appreciate it when concepts are explained simply and when illustrations highlight the text. Teacher-librarians with limited budgets often will opt for online products rather than text because of the availability for all students to access the online product at one time and because often these products allow students access to them while working from home. Many states have eased the burden of cost on many subscriptions by providing online subscriptions to schools as part of a state grant.

Public librarians do not have the same constraints as teacher-librarians in the schools, however. Often the public library has a larger budget and is able to purchase more materials. The public library knows it must contain information for all its patrons—from preschool children through adults. They usually have items at various reading levels. This is why wise teacher-librarians keep a good working relationship with their counterparts in the public library. Many times when students are unable to find necessary materials in the school's library, teacher-librarians are able to borrow books from the public library in order to satisfy the information needs of their student researchers.

Classroom teachers who are proactive and work closely with the teacher-librarian often have a big advantage. If the teacher-librarian knows that there is going to be a need for materials on a particular topic, she will make sure to use her budgeted funds to purchase additional materials on this topic for students to use. This is a case where "the squeaky wheel gets the grease." The teachers who are constantly in the school library communicating with the teacher-librarian usually have an advantage when it comes to getting books or materials purchased that support what they are doing in their classrooms. Many astute classroom teachers will actually bring titles to the attention of the teacher-librarian who is responsible for purchasing library materials. Teacher-librarians will go out of their way to make sure the LMC has the materials necessary, but advance plan-

ning goes a long way to ensuring that the materials will be there and ready when needed. If the teacher-librarian has advance notice about assignments, she will usually make sure that materials are available—even if she needs to borrow these materials from other schools or the public library.

This highlights an important issue when assigning research projects: the need to involve the teacher-librarian before making an assignment that will involve the use of the school library. Teachers need to be aware that teacher-librarians can often be the factor that makes an assignment successful. This is true because of the unique role the teacher-librarian serves in the school community and because the teacher-librarian has received special training in meeting information needs.

Teacher-librarians have a global view of the school. They usually know what research assignments are going on at any given time. They know what content is being covered at each grade level or in which class during each quarter or semester. They know what LMC materials will be used to support what is happening in the classrooms, and they know what is available for the students to use. For instance, the teacher-librarian knows that there will be a heavy demand on science materials for several weeks before the school science fair. She knows that if a sixth-grade class is doing a unit on poetry, it probably would not be a good idea for an eighth-grade class to study Walt Whitman unless the books containing his poetry are pulled and held back from the sixth graders.

Although numerous recent studies have demonstrated that student academic success is directly related to the presence of a qualified teacher-librarian in the school, many teachers are still reluctant to collaborate with the teacher-librarian and enlist her help when planning lessons or research assignments. Those teachers who involve their teacher-librarians in planning units or consult with them before assignments reap the benefits of the teacher-librarians' knowledge of information literacy and their experience with student researchers.

> Consult the website http://www.lrs.org/impact.asp for details on the studies demonstrating how school's library conditions affect student performance. A longitudinal study done in 2002 by the National Center for Educational Statistics showed that among 10th graders studied, those that performed in the middle and higher quartiles on standardized tests reported increased use of library resources for research. A copy of the results of the study can be accessed at http://nces.ed.gov/pubs2005/2005302.pdf.

Some school districts still do not draw on the expertise of teacher-librarians when developing curriculum. Why? Because teachers and administrators are not trained in their undergraduate (or graduate) education courses on how to best use teacher-librarians. This is unfortunate because often teachers' conceptions of the role of the teacher-librarian in the school or the teachers' understanding of how the teacher-librarian can assist them is based on an unfortunate experience they may have had themselves while using the library in junior or senior high. Many teacher-librarians are working hard to dispel any reservations that their colleagues may harbor about their ability to actually understand what is happening in the classrooms. As mentioned before, recent research on the value of the school library is helping. The American Association of School Librarians has published standards for teacher-librarians along with an Information Power initiative that is also helping to change the perception of the role that teacher-librarians fill in helping students learn. But not every teacher or administrator is on board, and many teacher-librarians still have a long way to go to become equal collaborators when it comes to curriculum and student achievement.

Below are some of the areas in which a teacher-librarian can assist classroom teachers and maximize the learning experience for students:

Scheduling:

- Teacher-librarians can let teachers know when other classes are going to be using the LMC sources that will be needed by their classes. This can prevent the demand on particular sources—for example, so that eighth-grade students doing a concerns paper and the seventh graders who are studying health do not need the books on eating disorders at the same time.
- Teacher-librarians know if students have conducted research on the same topic at another grade level and can help prevent the "recycling" of research papers at different grade levels—for example, keeping a paper on cancer done for a sixth-grade health class from reappearing as an eighth-grade concerns project.
- Teacher-librarians know the best dates when the LMC will be able to accommodate a class easily, allowing students' maximum usage of information sources. If ten sixth-grade classes and twelve eighth-grade classes have research papers scheduled during the month of April, there will be a strain on library materials, computer time will need to be shared by many students at the same time, and teacher-librarians will have less time to spend helping individual students.

Resources:

- Depending on the timeliness or complexity of the topic, oftentimes online or periodical sources are more helpful than books. Teacher-librarians can suggest which LMC resources will best suit the complexities of the research topics.
- Teacher-librarians receive hundreds of catalogs each year and are constantly looking for additional materials on topics students have researched in the past and new topics of recent interest. Teacher-librarians can purchase additional books on topics that are needed by students for research assignments. If they know in advance that these resources will be needed, they can be sure to get them purchased and processed before an assignment is given.
- Because public libraries and other libraries within the same school district are often willing to share resources with another school library that needs them, teacher-librarians can often secure additional materials from other libraries either before a class begins the research phase on a particular topic or they can often secure additional materials that are needed by individual students or teachers.
- Teacher-librarians are able to put materials that are to be used by many students on reserve or overnight checkout, so that the first five students who get to the LMC don't check out all the books needed by an entire class. Teacher-librarians can also limit the number of books a student can check out on a topic. This is particularly effective if several students are researching the same topic at the same time.

Instruction:

- Teacher-librarians can instruct students in important information literacy skills. They can guide students in how to extract information from the resources that are available to them in the school library, including print and electronic sources. They can also help students realize the proper and effective use of the Internet.
- Teacher-librarians can provide pathfinders on research topics.
- Teacher-librarians are familiar with several research models (e.g., Big6) and will instruct students and teachers in how to use a research model.
- Teacher-librarians can provide aids, such as bibliography sheets or Internet search forms, for research assignments.
- Teacher-librarians can pull materials from the LMC collection and group them in a specific location or on a cart for students to use without checking them out. They also can collect print materials for the teacher to check out and use in the classroom.

Collaboration:

- Teacher-librarians can suggest ways to improve assignments in order to involve students in more critical thinking and less information gathering.
- Teacher-librarians are able to help teachers assess the research part of assignments.
- Teacher-librarians can suggest possible rubrics to evaluate the research part of the assignment or they can actually help teachers develop rubrics.

There are several ways to collaborate with the teacher-librarians on research assignments. Talk to the teacher-librarian in your school as soon as you begin to plan an assignment. Using a collaboration form often helps classroom teachers and the teacher-librarian to look closely at the research project and the skills that will be needed for students to complete the assignment. A collaboration form helps to alleviate any confusion as to what students will be doing, what resources they will be expected to use, and what kind of information will be needed to complete the project. A collaboration form can also outline who will be responsible for each part of the assignment—who will teach the students to use the resources, who will evaluate the process, and what the students will need to know before embarking on the project. A sample collaboration form is provided in figure 2.1.

Approach your teacher-librarian for ideas on possible assignments that could be used with your class. Teacher-librarians know from previous experience what projects have been successful and which ones were duds. They often subscribe to listservs and periodicals that contain some creative ideas for research projects that have been shared. Teacher-librarians may have ideas on fun projects that include research. Language arts teachers are not the only ones who can find innovative research projects. Examples are available that can be used by teachers in many different disciplines, including mathematics.

Even if a formal collaboration form is not used, the teacher-librarian appreciates having a copy of the assignment and the rubric for assessing the project that was given to the students. Although this doesn't take the place of actual collaboration, it will help the teacher-librarian and any LMC staff to answer questions students may have about the assignment, it will alert LMC staff about library resources that can expect heavy use by students, and it gives LMC staff an idea of the time frame for the project. Often teachers think that their projects take priority over anything else that is going on in the LMC. When three classes are using the same information sources during the third week in April, fights can break out over who gets the books, kids grumble because they can't get on the computers, and the teacher-librarian has less time to help frustrated researchers find information. Finding out that no other classes have any research assignments the last week of March and the LMC could easily accommodate and service one of the

classes at that time makes the value of collaborating with the teacher-librarian very clear.

Research is an important activity that leads to developing those information literacy skills that students will use throughout their life. The emergence and popularity of the Internet has made the ability to extract needed and reliable information even more important. Making research fun will pay dividends. Not only will students acquire skills that will help them throughout life, but they will also increase their knowledge base on particular topics and become critical consumers of information. Planning ahead with the teacher-librarian can help teachers give their students positive research experiences and help them get a leg up on life.

FURTHER READING

For more information on how teachers and teacher-librarians can collaborate to improve student achievement, consult these books:

Buzzeo, Toni. *Collaborating to Meet Standards: Teacher/Librarian Partnerships 7–12.* Worthington, OH: Linworth, 2002.

Doll, Carol A. *Collaboration and the School Library Media Specialist.* Lanham, MD: Scarecrow Press, 2005.

Farmer, Leslie S. J. *Collaborating with Administrators and Educational Support Staff.* New York: Neal Schuman, 2007.

Grover, Robert, Carol Fox, and Jacqueline McMahon Lakin, eds. *The Handy 5: Planning and Assessing Integrated Information Skills Instruction.* Lanham, MD: Scarecrow Press, 2001.

Hughes-Hassell, Sandra, and Anne Wheelock, eds. *The Information-Powered School.* Chicago: American Library Association (ALA), 2001.

Kearney, Carol A. *Curriculum Partner.* Westport, CT: Greenwood Press, 2000.

Loertscher, David V., Carol Koechlin, and Sandi Zwaan. *Ban Those Bird Units!* Salt Lake City, UT: Hi-Willow Research, 2005.

Loertscher, David V., and Douglas Achterman. *Increasing Academic Achievement through the School Library.* Salt Lake City, UT: Hi-Willow Research, 2002.

Stanley, Deborah B. *Practical Steps to the Research Process for Middle School.* Englewood, CO: Libraries Unlimited, 2000.

Valenza, Joyce Kazman. *Power Tools Recharged: 125+ Essential Forms and Presentations for Your School Information Library Program.* Chicago: ALA, 2004.

For more information on the studies that have demonstrated a link between the school library media program and student achievement, consult:

Lance, Keith Curry, Marcia J. Rodney, and Christine Hamilton-Pennell. *How School Librarians Help Kids Achieve Standards: The Second Colorado Study.* San Jose, CA: Hi-Willow Research, 2000.

Lance, Keith Curry, and David V. Loertscher. *Powering Achievement.* San Jose, CA: Hi-Willow Research, 2003.

The Texas State Libraries website has sample collaboration forms at http://www.tsl.state.tx.us/ld/schoollibs/. The Indiana Department of Education has a website on teacher/librarian collaboration, complete with a sample collaboration form. It can be accessed at http://www.indianalearns.org/collaborativesheets .asp. For links to additional resources on collaboration, access http://eduscapes.com/sms/overview/collaboration.html.

Collaborative Planning Worksheet

Content Area	
Classroom Teacher	No. of students
Starting date	Due date

Library Media Center time needed	Pathfinder needed?

What do you want your students to know? What standards will be addressed?

How will students communicate their learning?	What library resources will be used?
Responsibilities: Teacher	**Responsibilities: SLMS**

***Remember to attach student handouts and rubric

Fig. 2.1.   Collaboration form.

3

Why Can't I Research UFOs?

Have you ever heard a teenage boy discussing his favorite football team? It's impressive. He probably knows the stats on every player, the team's strengths and weaknesses, the potential draft choices, and the team's chances of making it to the Super Bowl. How can he keep track of all that complicated information? Simple—he's motivated!

When students have a real interest in a specific topic, they are motivated to study it. Imposing a topic on students can be the kiss of death for an assignment, especially one that students are expected to focus on for several weeks. When roadblocks occur, when information is difficult to understand or even find, when the topics are ones they care nothing about, it is easy for students to get frustrated or lose interest. In order to complete the assignment, they may simply go through the motions and neglect any meaningful research. Or they may do everything they can to avoid doing the work completely—they may steal papers off the Internet or simply buy papers at one of the many sites available online. The more difficult or uninteresting the research topic becomes, the more the possibilities for plagiarizing increase. But if students really want to learn about something, there is nothing they won't do to dig for information.

Although students love to choose their own topics, they sometimes don't quite know what interests them. One year a colleague and I worked to make a meaningful research assignment, driven by the questions that students had about life in general; for example "Why is smoking bad for you?" or "How much television should you watch each day?" Then we gave the students free rein to choose their own topic and get started on research. The results highlighted some problems that can occur when teens have unlimited freedom to choose any topic. While some of our students' choices were excellent, others resulted in putting the student on shaky footing from the get-go. Some of the less work-

able topics chosen by students were ghosts, UFOs, and the Bermuda Triangle. Because these topics center on the paranormal, during their research students used lots of questionable sources and encountered the retelling of "authentic" stories. Although there was the potential for students to find information on the debunking of some of the stories, finding this type of information required the sophistication of skepticism that many middle schoolers do not possess. By the time my colleague and I realized that we had allowed students to choose topics that were doomed to be unsuccessful, we were already in the middle of the research process. This experience caused us to take a closer look at what we could do to avoid the problems our student researchers had encountered.

A well-chosen topic is the first and, arguably, the most important part of the research assignment. If a topic is poorly chosen, it can be the cause of numerous problems. Too much information, too little information, concepts that are too difficult to comprehend—each of these problems can be frustrating, boring, or daunting to even the most dedicated researcher. So what can teachers do to help students choose something that they will enjoy learning about and, at the same time, be worth knowing?

When my colleague and I created our less-than-successful research project, we began by having our students list questions that they had about the world. Many had excellent inquiries: "Why are people prejudiced?" "What can be done to protect the ozone layer?" "How can crime be prevented?" "Will there be a cure for AIDS?" It was apparent that eighth graders cared about their world. But we also noticed that some students were stumped when it came to asking questions. Sure, they had them. But they often had difficulty thinking of them when they were required to list them. Some other students had unanswerable questions. For example "Is there life after death?" is an excellent question. But while there is a multitude of religious interpretations to answer this question, no one can really say for certain! It was obvious this would not be a good research question.

After getting disappointing results from our student's first research experience, the next year I met with the teacher-librarian several months before the project began. I decided that I wanted students to learn about an issue that someone in the world faces every day. The teacher-librarian and I brainstormed a list of over one hundred topics, from capital punishment to homelessness. Categories included global, legal, social, sports, and health issues. We also wanted students to consider new issues concerning the media and new advances in technology, issues related to alcohol or drugs, and hot topics like prejudice, discrimination, and terrorism. Our goal was to find something to ignite the interest of every student. We also wanted to ensure that there would be enough accessible materials on these suggested topics, so that students would be able to complete a research inquiry and find adequate information on each topic in the school's library. An important part of this activity for me as the teacher was that it gave me some involvement in the topics that my students would choose to research. After reading many unsuccessful research papers, I have gotten a feel for those topics that don't work. I also do not want to read papers on certain topics, and this was my opportunity to eliminate some of those topics from consideration.

The results of my collaboration with the teacher-librarian resulted in a diverse list of suggested topics. A copy of the list that was given to my students and is shown in figure 3.1.

Students were then asked to choose a topic for research from the list. Because I felt the list was pretty extensive, and because I knew that research materials were available at levels appropriate for my students, I discouraged any topics that were not included on the list. Then the teacher-librarian and I went a step further. After handing out the list to the students, I took them to the school library for a "topic talk." In the LMC the teacher-librarian had a cart full of nonfiction books ready for us. These books delved into issues that were included as possible choices on the topic list. As she introduced each book, the teacher-librarian gave students a brief explanation of what each book was about. Most students enjoy hearing book talks, but introducing books this way is especially informative for student listeners. I often would hear them comment, "Wow! I never knew we had a book about that!" This topic talk helped many students decide on the topics they wanted to research. For example, many students are not familiar with organ donation. Students have seen commercials on television that have been produced by the state of Illinois urging drivers to indicate their willingness to be organ donors on their drivers' licenses. When the book

covering this topic was displayed, it caught the attention of some students, especially those who had seen the spot on television. This topic talk not only gets the class thinking about things they would like to research, but it also gives them a better idea of some of the issues that are important in the world.

Although I have had great success with the possible topic choices, I also know that it is important to revise this topic list from year to year. New concerns pop up every day and newspapers and magazines are constantly bringing new issues to the forefront. Books on many new topics are published each year. A few years ago, cloning was a very popular choice among my students, but there was little interest in terrorism. How times can change! For the I-search assignment in my language arts classroom, I gear the topic list to include topics related to global issues. Teachers in other disciplines, such as science or social studies, may want to choose topics that are related to what is being studied in their classroom. For example, a fellow social studies teacher has students do posters on events or issues that occurred during the Civil War. She gives the students several suggestions of topics to consider, such as medical care or the Battle of Gettysburg, and has them choose from these suggestions some aspect of the Civil War that they find interesting enough to want to research. This poster project provides these students with an in-depth look at some element of this important event in American history—one that they might not otherwise have learned from their textbook.

As has been mentioned before, a teacher's first task before assigning a research project is to meet with the teacher-librarian. Teachers who show up in the school library with a class of students and expect the library to be chock full of materials on American scientists, Inca ruins, or the Industrial Revolution, may be setting up their students and themselves for disappointment. On the other hand, speaking to the teacher-librarian in advance to discuss the topics your students will be researching can reap rewards. Advance planning with the staff in the school library can ensure a profitable experience for your students and fewer headaches for you. Teacher-librarians are trained to help researchers find what they need, and they often will aid student researchers by diversifying or clarifying their topic selections.

Teachers who expect their students to do research must also familiarize themselves with the available resources that students will use to find information. Many teachers rely completely on the knowledge of the teacher-librarian without actually examining the sources that are available in the LMC for student researchers. While the teacher-librarian may know what is available for students to use for information, the classroom teacher knows the student who will be using that resource. Because classroom teachers interact with their students on a daily basis, they often have a better under-

SUGGESTED I-SEARCH TOPICS

Global issues

World hunger
Use of energy sources
Biological or chemical warfare
Cloning
Pollution – air, water, noise, etc.
Nuclear waste

Ecology
Garbage
Overpopulation
Rain forests
Deforestation
Child labor

Legal issues

Gun control
Rights of the accused – rights of victims
Rights of teens
Death penalty
Prison
Prayer in schools
Euthanasia – assisted suicide
Sexual harassment

Crime & science (DNA testing, lie detectors, forensics, etc.)
Crime prevention
Teen violence – gangs
Police brutality
Drug testing

Social issues

Teens & sex – abstinence
Teen pregnancy – teen fathers
Dating violence – Date rape
Abortion
Homelessness
Grief – coping with death
Adoption rights – open vs. closed
Gender bias

Divorce & its effects on families
    Child custody
    Single parenting
Poverty
Welfare
Gambling
Lotteries

Alcohol and Drugs

Effects of drugs
Smoking
Drug abuse prevention
Drug abuse treatment
Alcoholism & its effects
Teen drinking – peer pressure

Prejudice & Discrimination

Prejudice – causes, effects, prevention
Hate crimes
Discrimination against certain groups:
    Elderly
    Poor
    Disabled or mentally ill
    Women
    Homosexuals
    African-Americans

Fig. 3.1. A copy of the list that was given to my students.

SUGGESTED I-SEARCH TOPICS

Health & Medicine

Eating disorders – anorexia or bulimia
Body image
Biomedical ethics
Chronic illness
Mental health

AIDS
Fetal alcohol syndrome
Organ donation
Alternative medicine
Animal testing

Sports issues

Cheating
Violence in sports
Gender equity
Sports & commercialism

Recruitment of athletes
Drugs & sports – steroids
Science & sports performance

Media & Technology

Advertising
    Persuasive techniques
    Alcohol advertising
    Should ads be aimed at kids?
Violence on TV
Sensationalism on TV
Values portrayed in TV, movies
Media & politics
Internet – positive or negative influence?
How technology will change
Virtual reality and its uses
Cyber crimes

Education issues

Equal opportunity
Trends in education
Science vs. religion in schools – creationism
vs. evolution
Censorship in the schools
Learning disabilities – ADD
Illiteracy

Miscellaneous

Immigration – past & present
Illegal immigrants
Animal welfare
Hunting

Food

Vegetarians, vegans, etc.
Fads, diets
Nutritional information & its effects on
  eating habits
Foods of different cultures
How safe is our food? – additives &
  engineering

Fig. 3.1. *Continued*

standing of how difficult some books may be for certain students to read and understand. Teachers also have a better idea of what types of books a particular student may find appealing. Teachers need to visit the school library and browse the shelves. Browsing not only will provide an idea of the range of books available on varying topics, but teachers may also get ideas of additional topics that would be good choices for their student researchers. If the teacher has a concrete idea of what print materials are available in the LMC for the students to use, she can be more realistic in her expectations and can guide the students to a more successful research experience. Teacher-librarians also rely on classroom teachers to point out areas where the school collection may be weak. Recommending titles that classroom teachers have found reviewed in journals or that they have read about helps the teacher-librarian as well.

Teachers should also not neglect the online sources. Currently teacher-librarians have directed budgets away from the purchase of print resources to allow for the purchase of more online products. These online resources have the advantage of being more current while also having reputable information. Becoming familiar with these resources is a task that every teacher should master.

When assigning the I-search project, I know it is important to let the students know up front what will be expected and the time frame for the project. It is not enough for me to introduce the project in the classroom. I find that students need a handout that introduces the project and also lets them know how much time they have to work on it. Figure 3.2 is an example of a handout I have used for my I-search project. This handout becomes part of an entire packet I put together for students. The packet also includes a Project Proposal Form and the rubric for the project. My students keep these handouts in their binders, and they refer back to them throughout the research process.

The Research Project Proposal (figure 3.3) serves several purposes. It requires students to do some serious thinking about their selection rather than just choosing a topic because a best friend has also chosen it. The proposal also requires that students justify why they have found their topic a worthwhile issue to explore. Students must also include questions that they will try to answer about the topic during the course of their information search. These questions will drive their research. The process of listing questions also helps me explain to students why some topics may be too broad for the assignment or why some topics may need to be expanded in order to make the research worthwhile. Students with too many questions may need to focus their research on a particular aspect of the issue they are researching. Students with too few questions may need to expand their topic a bit.

Finally, I require that students get a parent signature on the Project Proposal. This gets parents involved in this important learning activity. It serves notice to parents that a major project is assigned, so that they too can keep an eye on their child's progress. It also gives parents a chance to voice their opinion on the topic their child has chosen. Asking parents to sign off on the Project Proposal allows time for the child and the parent to negotiate any concerns at home before the research process even begins. It prevents students from having to change their topic midstream because of parent objections to the topic chosen by their child. It also gives parents a chance to help students with the questions that will drive their research. Having parents sign this project proposal gets them involved in the project timeline from the beginning.

Although this project proposal has worked well for me, I know other teachers who have effectively used a K-W-L form to get students focused in on their topic. The K-W-L form asks students to, first, think about and write down what they already know about their topic (What I Know). Then they must compose some questions they need to find out about the topic (What I Want to Know). Finally, students must list possible library resources they will use to "Locate" the needed information. These three inquiries form the K, W, and L of the form. Teachers have found this method an excellent way to get students focused on their topic and get them thinking about a plan of attack for finding the information they need to complete the assignment.

> More information on K-W-L can be found at the following websites: http://www.graphic.org/kwhl.html or http://www.learningpt.org/literacy/adolescent/strategies/kwl.php or http://www.ncrel.org/sdrs/areas/issues/students/learning/lr2kwl.htm or http://www.readingquest.org/strat/kwl.html. A printer-friendly version of a K-W-L chart is available at: http://www.ncsu.edu/midlink/KWL.chart.html or http://www.eduplace.com/graphicorganizer/pdf/kwl.pdf.

Whether a teacher-generated Project Proposal Form or a K-W-L chart is used, the important thing is that the students think about the topic they have chosen, consider why they feel it would be a good topic for research, and know where they can go to find information. Getting students to really think about the topic can yield dividends for the classroom teacher in that it forces students to become more focused on their task. I have had many students choose another topic after trying to fill out the project proposal. This is good, because the worst thing that can happen is to have a student spend a lot of time trying to research a topic only to discover he doesn't really like the topic he has chosen or that it is difficult to find enough information about it. Not only is this a waste of his time, it also sometimes causes the student to get behind in his research. Teenagers like choices and want to take ownership of what they do. It

FOURTH QUARTER
CONCERNS PROJECT

You have the opportunity,
the terrible freedom to learn.

CONCERNS … ISSUES … CHALLENGES

How did we get where we are today?
How has the past shaped our present?
How will we cope?
How should we manage the challenges of life that face our society today?
What is the best way to deal with these concerns?

EXPLORE AN ISSUE.
What do you find interesting?
surprising?
important?
upsetting?
encouraging?

DIG DEEPLY INTO YOUR CONCERN.
Find out all you can.
Then form opinions about the issue.

First, research your topic as thoroughly as possible. It is **strongly recommended** that you read a complete book on your topic. It is also recommended that you interview an expert or someone familiar with your issue. This will give you a deeper understanding of your issue.

We will spend about 3 – 4 weeks researching -- _____

You will then write an **I-Search paper** that discusses the importance of your topic, informs the reader about your topic, and explains your views on the topic and the conclusions that you have drawn through your research.

We will spend 2 weeks in class writing the paper -- _____

PAPER WILL BE DUE ON _____

Fig. 3.2.   A handout that I have used for my I-search project.

CONCERNS PROJECT PROPOSAL

Name _____ Date _____

What topic do you wish to study for your I-search project?

_____

_____

_____

What questions do you wish to answer about your topic? Be specific!

_____

_____

_____

_____

_____

_____

Write a few sentences explaining why you want to study this topic and why you believe it is a worthwhile topic.

_____

_____

_____

_____

_____

_____

****

For parents: Your signature indicates that you have reviewed the entire concerns project packet and that you approve of your child's topic.

Parent signature: _____

****

This topic has been approved by your teacher.

Teacher signature: _____

Fig. 3.3. The Research Project Proposal.

is better that the student be invested in the process from the beginning. We want the students to be enthusiastic about their topic, because this will be reflected in their projects, much to the delight of the teacher who has to assess their efforts.

FURTHER READING

For more information on the K-W-L method, consult the following:

Ogle. D. K-W-L: A teaching model that develops active reading of expository text. *Reading Teacher* 39 (1986): 564–70.

Rankin, Virginia. *The Thoughtful Researcher*. Englewood, CO: Libraries Unlimited, 1999.

For more information on possible topic choices, consult the following books:

McDougald, Dana. *100 More Research Topic Guides for Students.* Englewood, CO: Libraries Unlimited, 1999.

Whitley, Peggy J., and Susan Williams Goodwin. *99 Jumpstarts for Kids: Getting Started in Research.* Englewood, CO: Libraries Unlimited, 2003.

Whitley, Peggy, Catherine Olson, and Susan Goodwin. *99 Jumpstarts to Research: Topic Guides for Finding Information on Current Issues.* Englewood, CO: Libraries Unlimited, 2001.

4

This Sounds Hard!

After a student selects a topic and focuses on the questions he wants to answer through his research, the next step is for the student to determine exactly what he is expected to do to complete the project successfully. What will the final product look like? Will it be a paper? A poster? A podcast? A combination of all of these? Will the teacher determine the format of the final piece or will the student select it? How many sources is he expected to use? What kinds of sources? If the final project is a written piece, there is the inevitable question, "How long does it have to be?" It is only fair that teachers clearly state their expectations for the project and give their students a clear idea of what the finished product will look like so there will be no surprises. Two strategies have helped me clarify to my students what is expected of them: (1) to have them look over and analyze exemplary/model papers from previous classes, and (2) to present them with the assessment tools for the project before they begin their research.

EXEMPLARY/MODEL PAPERS

Using exemplary papers or projects from previous students are the best way to show kids where they're headed. When students can actually see an example from an earlier student, they have a visual model of the assignment. It gives the student a target to shoot for.

Of course, this won't work the first year you do a project. Instead of using exemplary papers or projects when an assignment is given for the first time, the teacher might want to do the assignment along with the class, step by step, in order to model the process and product for the students. This is an especially powerful strategy, for you as well as for your students. Modeling the process for your students gives them a window into the thinking, planning, and organizing that a multifaceted project entails. As you, the teacher, walk through the process and demonstrate the decisions that you make along the way, you create a climate of collegiality that invites students into the process. By engaging in the research process along with your students, you can better understand the challenges students may encounter.

Appendix A to this book contains a sample of an exemplary paper that a student created for an eighth-grade concerns project. This exemplary I-search paper is indicative of what I have come to expect from my students for this assignment. Although at first glance it may appear beyond the realm of what students can produce, it is not. Students who are given adequate time and teacher-directed instruction are able to produce a paper of comparable quality.

If you choose to use an exemplary model, begin by making copies of a couple of exemplary papers from previous years and hand them out to students. However, showing students a sample paper is not enough. Although students usually know a good paper when they see one, it is often difficult for them to identify the elements that make the paper exemplary. They may say things like "It's long" or "It has lots of big words in it." In order for students to meet the criteria for the project and produce a similar paper, students need to be able to identify the elements that make a piece exemplary.

So after my students read an exemplary model, I organize them into cooperative groups. Each group is given a question to consider as the group members read through the paper that they have received to review. Students are encouraged to highlight sections of the paper that give support to the question that they have been asked to consider. The following questions are examples of ones that I give to the students as they focus on the criteria that make the paper exemplary (included are possible responses from the students):

1. What kinds of information does the writer include about the topic? What evidence is there that the

writer looked at different aspects of the issue? (Students will notice that the writer included statistics, definitions, explanations, examples, and opinions from several sources.)

2. How is the paper organized? Are there sections? What are they? (Students will notice that there is an introduction, body, and conclusion. The body is divided into paragraphs, and each new paragraph deals with a subtopic.)

3. What evidence is there that the writer has thought about and analyzed the information found? (Students will notice that the writer has included his or her reactions and opinions on the topic and has presented different points of view with appropriate support. Because the paper is written in the first person, the writer is doing more than simply repeating information. The writer is thinking about the information, making connections, and forming opinions of his own.)

4. What evidence is there that the writer tried to interest the readers and get them to think about the topic? (Students will notice a strong lead and a thought-provoking conclusion. Writer's voice will be evident. Students will identify well-written sentences.)

5. Why did your teacher choose this paper as an exemplary one for you to read? (This is a broad question, and students can focus on any aspect of good writing that struck them as they were reading the exemplary model.)

After each group has had time to discuss the exemplary paper and formulate their responses to the question that their group has been given, we convene again as a class. Each group's findings are reported to the class as a whole and additional comments are encouraged from students in other groups. This discussion helps students better understand the elements that the teacher will be looking for in their final papers. This also gives the teacher an opportunity to teach about ideas, organization, voice, word choice, sentence fluency, and conventions. Because I consistently use a rubric that deals with these traits for all writing assignments, the students already have a pretty good idea about what they need to do to produce a paper that is comparable to the exemplary model that was read in class.

As the students move through the various stages of the research process, they can refer back to the exemplary models for ideas on how to construct their individual papers. When I first used exemplary models, I feared that students would slavishly copy the style of the sample we had discussed. I have been pleased to find that this seldom occurs. A very good paper can inspire a student to rise to the challenge, not settling for just good enough but often going beyond and creating a paper that can be used as an exemplary example the next year!

ASSESSMENT TOOLS

Once the teacher has determined the purpose and the student outcomes for the assignment, it is important to decide what form the assignment will take and how it will be assessed. What will the final product look like? The traditional term paper has served us well for many years and is still a worthwhile endeavor. In fact, the reason I take this "traditional" route to give my students experience with research is because it allows me to systematically teach and reinforce skills as students apply information literacy skills. I know that the I-search paper is not as "flashy" or technological as having students create a wiki or a PowerPoint presentation, but I do know that in the approach I have chosen, students really learn information literacy skills that can be applied to any project that demands the use of these skills—but you may wish to explore some other options. In fact, we discuss some alternatives to the term paper in a later chapter.

For a research project that spans a number of weeks encompassing a multitude of expected outcomes, assessment tools should take many forms. It is important to keep in mind that if you expect students to achieve outcomes, you must develop tools to assess whether those outcomes have been reached. Of course, you are the one who will assess the final product and make the determination whether your goals have been reached. And certainly, assessment does not necessarily mean grading. Assessment can take various forms—for example, checklists, observations, and student reflections.

Another thing to keep in mind is that if one of your outcomes is that students will employ important information literacy skills, it is important to assess how well they have used these skills and what they have learned during the process. Too often it is only the final product or paper that is assessed rather than the steps taken to produce that final product. Ensuring that students are mastering important information literacy skills is as important as considering whether they can communicate the results of their research.

Teens need guidance in knowing what will be assessed, so it is important that teachers let students know up front what will be required for the project and what assessment tool will be used for the project. Equally important, teachers need to be able to measure whether students are achieving the standard or learning outcome that the project is designed to address. The following describes several types of assessment tools that can be used:

Checklist Strategy

A checklist is simply a guide that helps students attend to all aspects of the research process. When given to students at the beginning of the research activity, the students know what the teacher wants the students to do for the project. A checklist can include elements for the process as well as the product. Figure 4.1 is an example of a checklist can be used for guiding research.

Rubric Strategy

A rubric is a scaled set of criteria that clearly defines for the student and the teacher what a range of acceptable and unacceptable performance looks like. Its purpose is to provide a description of successful performance. A crucial feature of rubrics is language that describes, rather than labels, performance. Evaluative words such as "better," "more often," and "excellent" do not appear in rubrics. Instead, the language must precisely define actions in terms of what the student actually does to demonstrate skill of proficiency at that level. An example is shown in figure 4.2.

Rubrics are an excellent assessment tool for a written piece, because a rubric can provide a student with the specifics needed to meet expectations. A well-written rubric gives writers a clear target to shoot for with no surprises. The rubric also becomes a guide for instruction by the teacher as well as a self-check tool for students as they revise their papers. I have had success adapting the six-trait writing rubrics designed by Vicki Spandel that are found in her book, *Creating Writers through 6-Trait Writing Assessment and Instruction*. I have created rubrics that focus on the essentials of good writing as well as the specific features present in a research paper, such as if the writer has included important and enlightening

Name_____ Period_____

Instructions: Student must have the teacher or teacher-librarian check off each box as each of the following phases of the research process is completed.

☐ I chose a topic on _____ that is interesting to me.

☐ I listed questions about my topic that I want to answer.

☐ I found information about my topic in at least two kinds of resources

☐ I took notes to answer my questions. My notes give important and complete information. I used my notes to write sentences about my topic.

☐ I assessed how well I completed the assignment.

Fig. 4.1.   An example of a checklist that can be used for guiding research.

Rubric Example for Process

Demonstrated indicator of student performance: Integrates new information into one's own knowledge.

- *Novice*: Puts information together without processing it.

- *Apprentice*: Integrates information for a variety of sources to create meaning that is relevant to own prior knowledge and draws conclusions.

- *Expert*: Integrates information to create meaning that connects with prior personal knowledge, draws conclusions, and provides details and supporting evidence.

Fig. 4.2. An example rubric.

details about the topic. Are facts and examples included? Is the paper structured in a logical, well-ordered style? Is there a strong, engaging lead? These elements are clearly stated within the traits of ideas and organization in the rubric. I have found the Spandel model is easy to "tweak" in order to include elements essential to a research assignment.

Figure 4.3 is an example of the rubric I have successfully used for my eighth-grade concerns project. In this rubric, I have chosen to have students concentrate on the areas of ideas, organization, voice, and conventions.

My students use the rubric while writing their first draft and also while revising their paper. I have found it is also helpful to teach mini-lessons on how to use the rubric. For example, I may want to do a mini-lesson to reinforce the trait of ideas. The rubric states that the writing should be "bursting with interesting tidbits that inform or expand the reader's thinking." During the mini-lesson on this element, students focus on making sure that their papers have those "interesting tidbits" that are needed by looking in their papers for statistics, quotes, or intriguing facts about their topic that will engage readers. The rubric in my example also states, "My beginning gives a hint of what is coming and makes you want to read on." During a mini-lesson on this element, students experiment with different leads until they create an opening that will draw readers into the paper.

A rubric not only keeps students focused on outcomes, it also keeps teachers focused and helps them to overcome bias. For example, I sometimes gravitate toward a paper on a topic I find interesting, such as homelessness, and be more generous than I should when I read a student's compassionate paper on this issue. On the other hand, I also have strong opinions on other issues, such as gun control or capital punish-

ment, which could get in the way of a fair assessment of a paper on one of these topics. I also know that I can become less than enthusiastic about reading a number of papers on the same topic, such as anorexia, a popular topic choice among female middle schoolers. A good rubric helps me focus on the individuality that each writer brings to the topic rather than my personal feelings on the topic itself. A good rubric helps me look beyond an attractive cover, distracting fonts, or the constant misspelling of a single word and keeps me focused on what really matters.

A rubric is also a godsend for helping parents understand the expectations of the project. Often parents want to help a student with an assignment but are not sure how to go about it. A rubric helps parents know what is expected for the project and can turn parents into allies in our efforts to guide students to improve their writing. If parents know that supporting opinions with facts is important, they will be looking for that in their child's paper. Another advantage is the element of "no surprises." When expectations are clearly stated up front, no parent can say that his child didn't know he had to . . . ., well, you get the picture!

Figure 4.4 is a rubric that evaluates an I-search paper as to how well the writer has organized the paper, researched the topic, created knowledge, involved the reader (always important when you have a hundred papers to grade), and the paper's freedom from grammatical errors.

Rubrics are great for providing students and teachers with guidelines for assessment. Just as important is looking at your rubric after assessing the assignment. Did the students meet the learning outcomes? If not, look at the rubric to see how it can be changed to improve student learning and the quality of the projects. In some cases, the rubric may be unclear or too rigorous.

RESEARCH PAPER 6-POINT RUBRIC

IDEAS	ORGANIZATION	VOICE	CONVENTIONS
6 My ideas are crystal clear and focused. I have insight and an in-depth understanding of my topic. I have thoughtfully selected researched details that are rich, significant, and accurate. My details are intriguing – not just things everyone knows.	**6** My paper has a thoughtful structure that guides the reader through the text. Super organization makes my ideas clear. The lead is unforgettable. Conclusion is enlightening and leaves the reader thinking. Transitions are satisfying and well-crafted.	**6** This is ME! It's as individual as my fingerprints. This paper begs to be read aloud. You want to share it. I love this topic! I don't overwrite, but I use my voice to keep readers hooked. My tone and flavor enhance my topic and purpose. A reader will find this paper tough to put down.	**6** Only the pickiest of editors will spot errors. I have shown that I have mastered a wide variety of conventions. I have correctly cited sources. The layout is enticing.
5 My paper is clear and focused throughout. I have a strong main idea. I used research to make my writing convincing and authentic. My main idea is expanded and well-supported with accurate details and evidence. I use important details.	**5** Order works well with my topic and my purpose. The structure is evident, but not too obvious. I have a lead that is interesting and inviting. My conclusion feels just right. I have smooth transitions.	**5** My voice is lively, expressive, and enthusiastic. The tone and flavor are right for my topic, audience, and purpose. I want my audience to like this topic and to tune in, and it shows in my writing.	**5** Any minor errors are easily overlooked. I did proofread carefully and it shows. I used good conventions to make my text easy to read. I have correctly cited sources. There is sufficient length and complexity to demonstrate a range of conventions appropriate to the writer's grade level. The layout is appropriate.
4 Most of my paper is clear and focused. It is easy to tell where this paper is headed. I have some great details. I might have some generalities and need to dig deeper. I need some more information to give a more complete and accurate picture.	**4** The order works – readers will not get lost. My structure is definitely there, but might be a little predictable. I have a lead and a conclusion that do the job. My transitions are there and are usually helpful.	**4** I show some sparks of individuality, enthusiasm, and spontaneity. Tone and flavor are acceptable for topic, audience, and purpose. I have some strong moments, but my voice comes and goes. My paper may not be unique.	**4** I made some noticeable but minor errors. It is readable but lacks close attention to editing. A more thorough once-over is needed before publication. Sources may not be cited accurately. Basics are OK. Layout is acceptable.
3 General information provides the big picture. I usually stick to my topic. Some "details" may be things that readers already know. Some information may be inaccurate. There might a lot of generalities, clichéd thinking, and filler. My topic might be too big. I need to "zoom in" more.	**3** Some parts may be out of order. I have a lead and a conclusion, but one or both of them may need work. Transitions may be unclear or may be too obvious and predictable. It might be hard to see how some of my ideas are connected.	**3** My writing is sincere. This sounds like an OK paper. My tone may not be a perfect fit for the audience, topic, or purpose. I seem distant from my audience. I don't think about my audience. I just write.	**3** There are a few noticeable, distracting errors. There are some errors on some basics, like periods and spelling. Errors occur in bibliographical citations. There may be some run-on sentences, comma splices, or errors in usage, grammar or verb tense. Thorough editing is needed. Layout may need some attention.
2 There is just a hint of a main idea. This is pretty sketchy. I didn't say much. Inaccurate information can confuse the reader. Factlets or tidbits may not support my main idea.	**2** Hard to follow! I seem to go in different directions. I don't connect ideas to my main point. Lead and/ or conclusion may be missing or dull. Transitions are unclear or missing.	**2** Sometimes I may sound like an encyclopedia. Sometimes I may sound too chatty. Tone and flavor are inappropriate. I don't sound like I care too much about what I am writing. I don't care about my audience too much.	**2** This has many errors. Some errors get in the way of meaning. Line-by-line editing is needed. Limited attention has been given to layout. Citations are inaccurate or missing.
1 These are just notes and thoughts. Readers will have to guess at a main idea. Inaccurate information.	**1** This is just a jumble of details and random thoughts. Nothing goes with anything else. There is no lead. It just begins. There is no conclusion. It just stops.	**1** Voice is missing from this paper. It does not sound like an individual wrote this paper. If I liked this topic or knew more about it, I could put more into it. The reader will probably be bored.	**1** Serious frequent errors make reading this extremely difficult. I need some help with editing. Citations are missing.

Fig. 4.3. An example of the rubric I have successfully used for my eighth-grade concerns project.

Name _____

I-SEARCH ASSESSMENT

	Needs Improvement	Somewhat Satisfactory	Satisfactory	Exemplary
ORGANIZATION Introduction – states the topic and why the topic is important Body–information is organized logically Conclusion–sums up the information and the writer's thoughts on the topic Traditional words or phrases are used appropriately				
THOROUGH RESEARCH Information is detailed, complete, and from a variety of sources Reasons and examples are given to support opinions and to explain the information stated Information and statistics are accurate Different sides of an issue are presented				
REFLECTIVE THOUGH The writer shows a thorough understanding of the topic The writer expresses his/her point of view on the topic				
INVOLVEMENT OF THE READER Paper is easily understood The lead gets the attention of the readers Questions or statements encourage the reader to think about the topic				
MECHANICS Paper is free of spelling or punctuation errors Paper is divided into paragraphs				
BIBLIOGRAPHY At least four sources are listed Sources are listed in correct format				

Fig. 4.4. A rubric that evaluates an I-search paper.

In others, you may need to make it more difficult. After using the rubric to assess your first assignment, you will become expert at seeing how changes in a rubric can change the nature and quality of student work.

When assessing a unit or assignment that requires information literacy skills, it is as important to assess the "process" (research) as it is to assess the "product" (final paper). One way to do this is to make sure the rubric or checklist includes assessments for both, giving equal importance to both process and product. An example of a checklist for an assignment that would include both an oral and written presentation is shown in figure 4.5.

The rubric in figure 4.6 is one that was successfully used for a sixth-grade I-search project. Notice that the rubric takes into consideration both the product and the process.

All of the rubrics and checklists modeled in this chapter can be adapted to fit other assignments. The important thing for teachers to understand is that a rubric or checklist is a guide for students, detailing what is expected for the assignment. Remember, it is not necessary to assess students on everything in an assignment. In one assignment you can assess a paper for conventions, in another assignment you can concentrate on voice. In an assignment involving research, the most important thing may be to assess how well students used information sources to get details for their paper or how many information sources they consulted. Before I used rubrics, I got all kinds of results when assignments were turned in. Incorporating rubrics and exemplary models into my instruction has allowed my students to become

The following websites provide templates for constructing rubrics: http://www.landmark-project.com/classweb/rubrics/4x4rubric.html and http://rubistar.4teachers.org. For more information on constructing rubrics, templates, and examples, the Discovery School site developed by Kathy Schrock at http://school.discovery.com/schrockguide/assess.html provides a list of valuable Web links. Http://www.sedl.org/loteced/opdc/resources/constructing_rubrics.pdf provides a list of things teachers should consider in constructing rubrics.

NAME:		
GRADING CRITERIA		

I. PROCESS	Possible Score	Your Score
Keyword list	10	
Bibliography sheet with 3 sources listed	15	
Notecards – minimum of 30	10	
Exit slip	15	
TOTAL POSSIBLE POINTS FOR PROCESS	50	

II. PRODUCT		
Visual		
Content	5	
Appearance	5	
Written presentation		
Organization	5	
Content	10	
Mechanics	5	
Oral presentation		
Organization	5	
Content	10	
Presentation	5	
TOTAL POSSIBLE POINTS FOR PRODUCT	50	

Fig. 4.5.   An example of a checklist for an assignment that would include both an oral and written presentation.

I-Search	Exceeds Expectations	Meets Expectations	Goal for Improvement
Proposal or Introduction	• Paper has a good lead that states topic • Describes what is known • Describes search questions	• Topic is stated • States what is known • States search question	• Topic is stated • Few ideas stated • Very few questions stated
My Search Process	• Sequence of steps described clearly • Details, feelings, and reactions described • Problems, good sources, additional help described	• Simple step-by-step format • Some details, feelings, and reactions included • Some problems sources, and help stated	• Steps to process are minimal • Details, feelings, or reactions stated insufficiently • Problems, sources, and help stated minimally
What Have I Learned?	• Focused on three or four major areas • Included details that answer questions stated in the proposal • Organized in a logical manner using good transitions	• Focus on one or two main areas • Limited number of questions answered • Evidence of transitions and order	• No clear focus • Very few questions answered from the proposal • Unorganized
What This Means to Me? (Conclusion)	• Described development as a researcher • Described which things meant the most • Described what affect this will have on you in the future	• Stated development as a researcher • Stated which things meant the most • Stated what affect this will have on you in the future	• No evidence that writer developed as a researcher • Meaningfulness not stated • No mention on what affect this will have on writer in future
Works Cited (Bibliography)	• Use of at least 5 different sources • References in alphabetical order • Correct format for each source	• Use of 3 or 4 different sources • 1 or 2 references out of order • Some errors in formatting sources	• 2 or less sources used • More than 2 sources out of order • Many errors in bibliographical format

Fig. 4.6. A rubric that was successfully used for a sixth-grade I-search project.

more successful in achieving the outcomes I want to see in their research and writing.

FURTHER READING

For more information on creating rubrics or checklists for writing assessment, consult:

California School Library Association. *From Library Skills to Information Literacy: A Handbook for the 21st Century.* 2nd ed. San Jose, CA: Hi-Willow Research, 1997.

Duncan, Donna, and Laura Lockhart. *I Search, You Search, We All Learn to Research.* New York: Neal Schuman, 2000.

Eisenberg, Michael, Carrie A. Lowe, and Kathleen Spitzer. *Information Literacy: Essential Skills for the Information Age.* 2nd ed. Westport, CT: Libraries Unlimited, 2004.

Phillip, Cyndi. Clear expectations: Rubrics and scoring guides. *Knowledge Quest* (November–December 2002): 26–27.

Rickards, Debbie, and Earl Cheek Jr. *Designing Rubrics for K–6 Classroom Assessment.* Norwood, MA: Christopher-Gordon, 1999.

Spandel, Vicki. *Creating Writers through 6-Trait Assessment and Instruction.* 4th ed. Upper Saddle River, NJ: Pearson Education, 2005.

Stiggins, Richard J. *Student-Involved Classroom Assessment.* 3rd ed. Upper Saddle River, NJ: Merrill Prentice Hall, 2001.

5

I Don't Know Where to Start!

Developing and using a project proposal is an effective method of getting students in the research mind-set because it forces student to develop questions about their topics. But students can have difficulty thinking of questions. Their first inclination is to ask about numbers. How much? How many? How big? But when researching most topics, real learning requires more depth. Students need to think of questions that lend themselves to digging more deeply into the why and how, the cause and effect, the pro and con.

Another problem with creating questions is that often some background information or summary knowledge about the topic is needed in order to develop intelligent and worthwhile questions. For example, if I were asked to create a list of questions on nuclear physics, I'd be stumped. Since I know absolutely nothing about nuclear physics, I would be hard pressed to come up with any questions beyond the obvious one of "What is nuclear physics?" Students may begin with basic questions about their topic, and as their knowledge about the topic grows, students may develop new questions. Therefore, students cannot be expected to have all of their questions figured out before the research process begins. Instead, they should be encouraged to develop more and more avenues of inquiry as they learn more about their chosen topic.

I have found that the best way for students to begin a research project is not to gather a big pile of stuff on their topic or to skim a book or other source for isolated facts or snippets of information. Instead, I ask my students to check out a nonfiction book on their topic and to read it cover to cover. Other than their school textbooks, students have rarely read a complete nonfiction book. And how many students really read their history or science textbook cover to cover over the course of a school year?

There are several benefits that students gain from reading a complete nonfiction book on their topic.

First of all, reading a complete book gives readers a deeper insight into their chosen topic and a better understanding of the concerns and controversies related to the topic. A book on gun control, for example, may explain how and why the writers of the Constitution included the right to bear arms and may trace this debate through to current times. It would also explain both sides of the gun controversy by detailing differing arguments and citing examples to illustrate various viewpoints. By reading such a book cover to cover, a student could more clearly see the various aspects of the controversy and form an educated opinion about gun control.

Another benefit of reading a nonfiction book is that it exposes readers to a genre they have probably had little experience reading. Nonfiction is important! Think of the reading that adults do on a daily basis. In order to get information about our world, our nation, our health, our careers, we read nonfiction in the form of newspapers and magazines, both in print and online. Developing nonfiction reading strategies is essential to literacy and is too often overlooked in our classrooms. Summarizing information, determining importance, and recognizing bias are essential strategies that need to be taught and practiced in order to develop able independent readers. Assigning a nonfiction book on their topic allows me time to teach students these strategies and helps my students develop critical reading skills.

An additional benefit of assigning nonfiction is that it often appeals to reluctant readers who are uninterested in fiction. Those students who roll their eyes at the suggestion of reading a story are often eager to read "true" books. Most importantly, students are eager to gather facts about a topic they truly care about.

Often the only nonfiction that students read is a textbook. Have you ever seen a student eagerly open his science or history textbook and get lost in its content?

I doubt it! Textbooks are not reader-friendly. Their format tends to be packed with information but often the writing is dull and stilted, lacking a clear voice. Yet in our school's library there is a wealth of engaging nonfiction literature available. Students need only browse the nonfiction shelves to find books that are filled with rich language, compelling description, entertaining details, dramatic photographs and illustrations, and clear explanations. Writers like Jim Murphy, Russell Freedman, James Cross Giblin, and Milton Meltzer are just a few authors who have written well-researched, well-crafted nonfiction books. Teacher-librarians are constantly reading book reviews and selecting new nonfiction titles to purchase for the school library collection. In addition, there are yearly awards and lists of the best nonfiction titles that can help teacher-librarians select good nonfiction choices. One excellent bibliography of nonfiction titles is the VOYA Nonfiction Honor List, an annotated list of books that is published in the magazine each August. Teachers who go to the school library and browse the collection of new nonfiction books will discover worthwhile nonfiction.

One of the recent trends in publishing that makes nonfiction books so attractive to students is the use of more graphics and color. Instead of reading a book that consists mainly of black text on a white page with possibly some grainy photographs, those nonfiction books that have combined colorful graphics with well-written, interesting facts have received a popular response from both students and librarians and have alerted publishers to the advantages of presenting important information in a colorful pictorial format. Now nonfiction titles burst forth with full-page illustrations, digitally enhanced photos, and engaging text. Students have a multitude of books that are so graphically intense that it doesn't seem like a chore to read them at all. Although these well-illustrated books may appear juvenile in scope, most are extremely well written and contain enough valuable information to give researchers a good overview of their topics. Although adults often dismiss the books in the juvenile section of the library, books published for younger readers have proved their worth as an excellent source for quick and accurate information on many topics. Would someone rather read a 500-page tome on a topic or a 100-page book on the same subject that is filled with interesting illustrations? Without a doubt, it seems easier to remember the information in a short book than that in a boring one. The idea of a well-crafted research project is to engage students and make research fun. Well-written nonfiction books that skillfully combine important facts with colorful illustrations do this.

I encourage students to be thoughtful about the nonfiction books they choose to read. A key element of a book intended for student use is its readability level. Sure, there may be several books on nuclear fission, but unless one is written at an elementary enough level for the concepts to be easily understood, the book will be useless to a person who has no idea what nuclear fission is. Finding a book geared to the readability level of slower readers enhances the possibility that they will actually read it. In addition, books that include a glossary of terms will save readers the effort of looking up the meaning of words that are unfamiliar.

Books covering scientific or technology topics must be current and filled with up-to-date information on the newest discoveries in these ever-changing fields. Because new discoveries and innovations are occurring daily, I encourage students to choose books with copyrights within the past eight years, five if it is a science topic, to ensure that the information they are getting is not outdated.

A reading workshop setting is a successful way for students to dig deeply into their nonfiction books. After going to the library to check out books, I schedule several class periods for sustained reading and note taking. I make sure that this sustained reading takes place in the classroom, where it is easier to create an atmosphere conducive to silent reading, away from the computers, constant movement, and large tables in the school library that often distract students from the task at hand.

Often students want to simply skim a book with a pen in hand for note taking. I discourage this practice, instead instructing students to read a chapter or, at least, several pages of their book without taking notes. After reading, I ask them to write down what they most want to remember from that chapter or section. What did they think was most important? Why? By saving the note taking until a complete chapter has been read, students are more able to determine what is most important. If students read with pen in hand, they often fall into the trap of writing down almost everything they have read. After all, since the information is new to them, it all seems important! It is easier to extract just the right kernels of information when a reader has more of the big picture that can be gotten from reading an entire chapter. This method also helps students because it discourages wholesale plagiarism.

Once students have read a complete book on a topic, they have learned quite a bit! Often after completing a book about a controversial topic, students are chagrined to discover that they are more ambivalent about where they stand on an issue. As their teacher, I am delighted to see this! It shows that they have been open to many aspects of an issue and can see the advantages, disadvantages, strengths, and weaknesses of their position. Their confusion shows that they are thinking deeply and recognizing that there is often no definite black or white answer but that many issues have a lot of gray areas. After the nonfiction book is read and they have gained valuable background into the topic they have chosen, students are now ready to revisit their project proposal and the list of original questions that they had about their topic. First, they see which questions they have answered. Next, they add more questions that have been prompted by their reading. These new questions give direction to their continued research.

FURTHER READING

For more information on using nonfiction books to drive student research, consult the following sources:

Carlson, Christine. Using nonfiction books to launch a successful research project. Young Adult Literature in the Classroom: Reading It, Teaching It, Loving It, edited by Joan B. Elliott and Mary M. Dupuis. Newark, DE: International Reading Association, 2002.

Daniels, Harvey, and Steven Zemelman. *Subjects Matter: Every Teacher's Guide to Content-Area Reading*. Portsmouth, NH: Heinemann, 2004.

Harvey, Stephanie. *Nonfiction Matters*. York, ME: Stenhouse, 1998.

Harvey, Stephanie, and Anne Goudvis. *Strategies That Work*. 2nd ed. York, ME: Stenhouse, 2007.

6

I'm Not a Good Researcher

There was an amusing television commercial that featured a family sitting down to a good, nutritious breakfast in their home's kitchen. Everyone is well groomed and happy to be going off to school or work. Then, suddenly the announcer shouts, "Get real!" and the picture of the refined and happy family dissolves into one where there is mass confusion, everyone is rushing around, and things aren't absolutely perfect. I think this commercial demonstrates what teachers "expect" and what teachers actually "find" when their classes go to the library media center to begin research. Teachers often think that bringing their classes into the school's library means that students will get right down to work to find information and begin taking notes, working without disturbing others. After all, students have been going to the library forever. They know what to do! The whole experience will be pleasant for everyone and a welcome break from what goes on in the classroom.

However, after many years of observing classes doing research in school library, I have found that what teachers are more likely to find is mass confusion. One student wanders aimlessly through the stacks looking for books. Another student, like the prehistoric hunter-gatherer, is pulling every book on organ donation, preparing to stack them in front of him on the library table. Another classmate is using the Internet and is typing into Google: "I need some information on gun control." Others are busy at the computers, industriously jotting down call numbers from the online catalog. A very few students are actually planning out their search, deciding what sources will be the most useful for finding needed information before they begin. Often students appear to be unfocused as they search for anything on their topic that could be useful.

I have found that if I prepare my students in the classroom before taking them to the LMC to begin note taking for their research, they fare much better. This preparation can make all the difference between a posi-

tive research experience and a negative one. One of the reasons kids hate doing research is because they haven't been trained how to systematically go about using their time in the LMC effectively. When students are not prepared for research in the school library, they spend time there spinning their wheels, trying to look like they are actually working, while instead they may be planning next weekend's activities or bonding with their friends. Instead of spending valuable LMC time actually working, some students are hoping that Mom or Dad will bail them out at home instead.

There are several things classroom teachers can do to prepare students for a successful research experience before they actually bring the class into the school library. The foremost suggestion is one that has already been discussed: Plan ahead with the teacher-librarian. Fortunately, the role of the teacher-librarian has evolved. Instead of being the "keeper of the books," the teacher-librarian is now a full partner with the classroom teacher in helping students acquire those important information literacy skills that will ensure lifelong learning. Nobody in the school better knows what is available in the LMC for students to use. The teacher-librarian also knows how to use these LMC resources effectively and can teach student researchers how to extract information from the variety of resources available there. In fact, a trained teacher-librarian is anxious to share research knowledge with students (and teachers). Teaching others how to use the resources in the LMC is her expertise. In fact, the teacher-librarian would rather teach students how to use the resources as part of an assignment. In contrast, teaching these important information literacy skills in isolation outside the context of an actual assignment means that students may fail to remember how to use Infotrac or Newsbank when they actually have an assignment and need to use these resources.

Classroom teachers should not assume that their students know how to use all of the information sources available in the school library just because they have been using the library since elementary school. The teacher-librarian will be the best judge as to how familiar students are with the LMC and its resources. In addition, the teacher-librarian will know what information skills may need to be taught or retaught as part of a research project.

Teacher-librarians have found that a student can never get enough practice using a particular information source that is available in the school library. It is amazing how easy it is for students to forget how to find information from grade to grade when they are not using research skills on a daily basis. Sure, kids learned about Infotrac in sixth grade. That doesn't mean they will remember it is available or will recall how to use it when they get to eighth grade—especially if they didn't use it the year before or if they weren't paying attention when it was first introduced. The computer-based sources to which the library subscribes may change from year to year. The way some of these sources look can change. New students transfer in every year—in growing districts, it seems like every day—and they often are ignorant of the information sources available in their new school. The teacher-librarian knows these things, so don't be surprised if she insists on scheduling time to teach the information literacy skills to your students as part of their research time in the school library. To get an idea of the scope of some of the information sources available to students when they need to research a topic, look at figure 6.1.

Although learning how to use information sources is a critical piece of research, learning how to research— the actions used in finding, recording, and publishing the results of research—is just as important. This is why I suggest that schools choose an information skills process model and have the school or district adopt it. What's an information skills process model? It is a systematic and organized way of researching and learning. You may know it better by the name information literacy model. Several of these exist, among them Eisenberg and Berkowitz's Big6 skills, the Handy 5, or the PLUS model used in Great Britain and Australia. Since teachers and librarians now have published guides with instructions on using these research models, it has become much easier to teach students the steps involved in creating a research project. A listing of sources describing the different information skills process models can be found in the bibliography to this chapter.

If your school does not have a prescribed information literacy model to follow, one should be chosen by the teacher assigning the research. If the entire school district

> A discussion of several information skills process models can be found on this site: http://www.big6.com/2002/03/26/research -foundations-of-the-big6%e2%84%a2-skills/. Information on the Big6 can be found on their website, http://www.big6.com.

can choose a model, the students can use the model from elementary through high school. Having this continuity is important, in that these skills can be reinforced at each grade level. In fact, individual states have published entire handbooks for their teachers with the approved information skills process model that they expect to be taught and used throughout their schools. A useful example of a statewide model is found in *The Handy 5: Planning and Assessing Integrated Information Skills Instruction*. Developed by the Kansas Association of School Librarians Research Committee, this book details the process students should follow when confronted with an information need and also includes sample lessons for teaching the process. Particular attention is given to tying the information literacy model to state standards.

Many schools make bookmarks of the steps involved in the research process model and have them available for students. Often, just having the steps involved in the model in front of them helps students refocus if they get off track during the research process. With enough practice, these steps will become ingrained, thus becoming part of the way students approach any problem, both in school and out. No matter which information skills process model your school chooses to use, all emphasize basically the same things, as all models describe a thoughtful approach on how to conduct research. In addition, when students are taught an information skills process model, they are more likely to know what to do when the class is brought into the school library to begin research.

> Lesson plans for teaching information literacy can be found at http://www.sldirectory.com/libsf/resf/libplans.html. The website http://www.informationliteracy.org/ also has links to sample lesson plans that aid in teaching information literacy skills.

Providing students with a checklist that they can fill out as they move through the project is another way of preparing them for the research experience. Figure 6.2 is an example of an assignment organizer I developed to fit a careers project. This assignment organizer gets the students to think about their research project and allows them to plan how they will attack the task before they actually get to the school library to begin looking for information. This example also reminds students of what is involved in the assignment and how the students will need to present their research results.

Teachers can find models of other student research organizers in the books mentioned in the bibliography to this chapter. Most astute teachers can adapt one of the organizers to fill their own needs or they can ask the teacher-librarian for help in putting a student research organizer together.

Giving the organizer to students before sending them to the school library to begin research helps my students

Where do you go to find information?

Print sources
Reference books
- General encyclopedias
- Subject encyclopedias
- Almanacs
- Atlases
- Dictionaries

Books
- Online catalog

Indexes
- National Geographic Index

Vertical file

Electronic sources
Online sources
- Online encyclopedias
  - *Britannica*
  - *Grolier*
- Student Resource Center
  - *Infotrac*
  - *Discovering Science*
  - *Discovering U.S. History*
  - *Discovering Authors*
- Daily life online
- Cobblestone online

CD-ROMs
- Career Discovery
- Career Cruising

Internet & World Wide Web

Multimedia Sources
- Videos & DVDs
- PowerPoint presentations
- Television programs

Personal sources
- Interviews
- Letters & E-mail

Fig. 6.1. Information sources.

CAREER RECRUITER BROCHURE

NAME _____

Today there are many choices of careers for people to consider. You are a recruiter for a particular profession. It is your job to convince others to consider your profession as a career. Your task is to create a brochure that will educate others about your profession and to persuade them that this is a career worth choosing.

Your brochure must:
- describe the career, including its responsibilities and activities.
- show the advantages and positive aspects of the career.
- have correct spelling, punctuation, and grammar.
- have a bibliography, correctly formatted.
- be attractive.
- be neat.

Career chosen for this brochure: _____

Questions that your brochure will answer about this career:

1. _____

2. _____

3. _____

4. _____

You must use at least two sources to find answers to these questions as well any other information you include in your brochure.
Take notes on the notecard forms and keep track of your sources by using the Bibliography Sheet.

Then plan and design your brochure.

Cover can be done on either construction paper or white paper.

Inside of brochure should contain information presented in an appealing and convincing manner and a bibliography, <u>correctly formatted.</u>

Fig. 6.2. Career brochure assignment organizer.

An excellent checklist developed by Barbara A. Jansen, a librarian at St. Andrew's Episcopal Upper School in Austin, Texas, that guides students through all steps of the research model can be found at http://www.ischool.utexas.edu/~bjansen/ Big6%20Instructional%20Unit%20Planning%20Guide.doc. An example of an online assignment organizer can be found at http://www.ri.net/schools/East_Greenwich/research.html. An interactive research process checklist based on the PLUS model can be found at http://www.mhs.vic.edu.au/home/ library/infoproc/index.htm.

focus on what they need to do. It gives them a road map that guides their activities throughout the course of the project. The assignment organizer helps them in the LMC, at the public library, at home on the Internet, or anywhere they do research. With an organizer to guide them, no student will be able to come up at the end of the project and say, "But I didn't know how to get started or what to do. I'm just not a good researcher!"

A keyword list is another thing my students work on in the classroom before beginning their search for information in the school library. This keyword list includes words related to the topic that the student has chosen to research. These are the words that can be plugged into indexes and databases when searching for needed information. Like the questions that students want to answer about their topic, a keyword list will change and amplify as students work through their research. When kids tell me they are having difficulty finding information, I often will ask them what search term they were using to find information. Lots of times students will get hung up in finding information because they just aren't looking under the right word. Often it is as simple as looking under "waste" rather than "garbage." Sometimes researchers need to try several different keywords before they locate the information they need. There are differences in terms from region to region. For example, when I attended college in another state and someone asked me the location of the "bubbler," I was dumbfounded. After I realized this person was looking for a water fountain, I was able to help her. Having lots of possible keywords ensures that students will find information. Figure 6.3 is an example of a handout that can be given to students to help them develop their own keyword list.

Name _____

Keyword List
My Topic is:

Other ways to say it	Larger topic that includes yours	Smaller topic related to yours	Persons, places, terms associated with your topic

Look for these words in an INDEX. Indexes can be:
- In the back of a book
- Online catalog
- Magazine/newspaper database
- Search engine

Fig. 6.3. Keyword list.

Teachers who desire successful research projects know it is important to allow students plenty of time to learn how to use the tools they need to create a worthwhile project. One of the first sources any student wants to use is the Internet. Instead of fighting this trend, I make sure the students are prepared to use the Internet effectively.

Students know about search engines but often are not savvy when it comes to using them. Students often don't know the difference between a search engine, a subject directory, and the invisible Web. They need instruction on ways to use the full value of the Internet. Taking time to teach or review Internet strategies that help students refine their searches means that instead of wasting time "Googling" for information, students can tailor their inquiries to be more focused.

> For good lesson plans about teaching Internet searching and safety, consult the following websites: http://www.cybersmartcurriculum.org/home or http://webquest.sdsu.edu/searching/fournets.htm.

It is also important for students to learn how terms can be combined for a Boolean search. Boolean searches are ways to combine terms using common terms "and," "or," and "not" to narrow a search. This is especially critical when using the Internet where a simple search can yield hundreds (or thousands) of hits. Students need to know when and how to combine terms that they have included on their keyword list in order to get the information that they need and eliminate the time spent searching though hundreds of search engine hits that have nothing to do with the information they are seeking.

Students need to know the differences on how to type in their terms in the search engine, subject directory, or online database that they have chosen to use. If I'm looking for information on how guns are used in crimes, I know I need to type in "guns crime" when I use Google, or "+guns +crime" when I use Alta Vista. I have to remember to put quotations around "Boston Tea Party" so that I get information about the historical event and not recipes. Examples of forms that will aid students in a search for their keywords in Internet search engines or subject directories can be found in many of the books mentioned at the end of this chapter. Adapting one of these forms into a student handout can save students valuable time when searching for information on the Internet.

Using a nonfiction book as the starting point for the research project can also be a real timesaver for students when it comes to research. I have found that all of my students are usually able to find one or two books on their topic in the school library. But after they finish with them, they often don't know where to go next for more information. The teacher-librarian and I spend time with each class, encouraging the students to look more closely at the nonfiction books that they have chosen to read. With a little instruction, students have learned to use the different parts of the nonfiction book that they have read to find information about other sources they can use during their research quest. For example, looking at the verso (or the back) of the title page in the book can give students additional clues as to where more books on the subject can be found. This page usually contains the Library of Congress cataloging-in-publication data (or CIP), bibliographic information that includes subject headings under which you can find the book. When students type these important subject headings into the online catalog or online databases, they often find additional materials on the topic they are researching. These subject headings then become additions to their keyword lists for the project. Some of the newer nonfiction titles include useful bibliographies, leading students to not only additional books on their topic but also periodical articles and websites as well. If a student is astute enough to have chosen a book with an up-to-date bibliography, the time saved by using the ready-made list, rather than trying to track down sources independently, can save the student valuable time and effort.

With proper preparation in the classroom, students will use their research time in the school library well. There may still be several students who feel the need to gather books, those who want to socialize rather than get down to work, and several who will still look lost, but preparing students for their research experience beforehand frees the teacher to give guidance to those students who don't know where to begin, how to keep track of the information they do find, and how to turn their research efforts into a cohesive project. When students are focused on a research path, when they have a list of possible keywords to search, and when trained teacher-librarians have the time needed to instruct students in important information skills and how to use the resources available to them in the school library, the whole process of gathering information becomes an exciting adventure in learning. It also makes for a much more organized and enjoyable class activity for everyone involved.

FURTHER READING

Additional information on information skills process models can be found in the following books:

Blume, Sheila, Carol Fox, Jacqueline McMahon Lakin, Betsy Losey, and Jan Stover, eds. *The Handy 5: Planning and Assessing Integrated Information Skills and Instruction.* 2nd ed. Lanham, MD: Scarecrow Press, 2007.

Eisenberg, Michael B., Robert E. Berkowitz, Robert Darrow, and Kathleen L. Spitzer. *Teaching Information Technology*

Skills: The Big6 in Secondary Schools. Worthington, OH: Linworth, 2000.

Eisenberg, Michael B., Carrie A. Lowe, and Kathleen Spitzer. *Information Literacy: Essential Skills for the Information Age*. 2nd ed. Westport, CT: Libraries Unlimited, 2004.

Grover, Robert, Carol Fox, and Jacqueline McMahon Lakin, eds. *The Handy 5: Planning and Assessing Integrated Information Skills Instruction*. Lanham, MD: Scarecrow Press, 2001.

Kuhlthau, Carol Collier. *Teaching the Library Research Process*. 2nd ed. Lanham, MD: Rowman & Littlefield, 1994.

Langhorne, Mary Jo, ed. *Developing an Information Literacy Program K–12*. New York: Neal Schuman, 1998.

Thomas, Nancy Pickering. *Information Literacy and Information Skills Instruction*. Englewood, CO: Libraries Unlimited, 1999.

Yucht, Alice H. *Flip It! An Information Skills Strategy for Student Researchers*. Worthington, OH: Linworth, 1997.

Additional information and suggestions on teaching students information literacy skills can be found in the following books:

Birks, Jane, and Fiona Hunt. *Hands-On Information Literacy Activities*. New York: Neal Schuman, 2003.

Harmon, Charles. *Using the Internet, Online Services, and CD-ROMs for Writing Research and Term Papers*. New York: Neal Schuman, 2000.

Herring, James E. *The Internet and Information Skills*. London: Facet, 2004.

Iowa City Community School District and Mary Jo Langhorne. *Developing an Information Literacy Program*. New York: Neal Schuman, 2004.

Koechlin, Carol, and Sandi Zwaan. *Build Your Own Information Literate School*. San Jose, CA: Hi-Willow Research, 2003.

Loertscher, D., and B. Woolls. *Information Literacy: A Review of the Research*. 2nd ed. San Jose, CA: Hi-Willow Research, 2002.

Rankin, Virginia. *The Thoughtful Researcher: Teaching the Research Process to Middle School Students*. Englewood, CO: Libraries Unlimited, 1999.

Riedling, Ann Marlow. *Learning to Learn: A Guide to Becoming Information Literate*. New York: Neal Schuman, 2002.

Ryan, Jenny. *Information Literacy Toolkit: Grades 7 and Up*. Chicago: ALA, 2001.

Stanley, Deborah. *Practical Steps to the Research Process for High School*. Englewood, CO: Libraries Unlimited, 1999.

Stanley, Deborah. *Practical Steps to the Research Process for Middle School*. Englewood, CO: Libraries Unlimited, 2001.

Valenza, Joyce Kazman. *Power Tools: 100+ Essential Forms and Presentations for Your School Information Library Program*. Chicago: ALA, 1998.

Valenza, Joyce Kazman. *Power Tools Recharged: 125+ Essential Forms and Presentations for Your School Library Information Program*. Chicago: ALA, 2004.

7

I'll Get It Done the Night before It's Due

Like most teachers, I have found that research projects come with their own set of class management issues. Every class is different and every student unique, so with five sections of eighth graders I can have approximately 125 challenges. I find myself dealing with the academically talented, the learning disabled, the struggling reader, the literal thinker, and both auditory and visual learners. And these aforementioned students are just some of the educational challenges. But do the following students also sound familiar? How about the hard worker, the disorganized, the procrastinator, the life of the party, the socialite, the unmotivated, the easily distracted, and the quiet one? How can I keep track of all these students, with their varieties of learning styles, abilities, personalities, and interests?

During the course of my I-search concerns project I have had to devise ways of keeping track of my students' progress to make sure that everyone is on track, industriously working, and not waiting until the night before to get cracking. Prior to the project I put together a student packet that includes an introductory page that lets students know up front just how much time will be spent on the I-search project. On this introductory page there is a space where the student needs to write in the date the I-search paper will be due. I don't just assign the project and let them loose. I also make sure that my students are aware that I expect to be monitoring their progress during this time; by allowing them class time to work on the project, I can keep them on track. In my packet I do not include a calendar, but I know other teachers who do. On the calendar they have plotted out the date the project proposal is due, the dates they will be researching in the school library, when the students are expected to begin work on their paper, and the date their paper is due. Figure 7.1 is an example of a calendar for a sixth grade I-search assignment.

When it is time for students to actually begin looking for information on the topic they have chosen, I bring

my classes to the school library. There, the teacher-librarian takes the necessary time to teach the important information literacy skills that the students need to learn in order to complete their research. After students become familiar with the information sources that are available for their use, these same students actually have to start working, researching on their own, and taking notes. This is when the phenomenon of "gathering" occurs. Students feel compelled to pile up as much information on their topic as possible. Busy researchers visit the bookshelves, grabbing every book they can on their topic. Next, they try the online periodical indexes, trying to locate a number of magazine articles on their topic. Then, they may surf the Internet, zipping through numerous sites related to their topic. All this activity makes it look like they are being very industrious. After all, they are buzzing around the library and piling up tons of sources. And while the stack of books and materials in front of them is increasing, while lots of articles are being identified, and while printers are churning out pages of text, one thing is not occurring: They are not actually reading the material they have located!

I have found it important to set the rule: "One source at a time." I insist that students read the information found in one source before moving on to another. And I encourage students to really read the information, not to just skim it or flip through it! Piling up material is counterproductive and inhibits others from using the same source.

I know sixth-grade teachers who have found another way to make sure that students use many different information sources and actually learn to use these tools before they begin a search for information. These teachers have the teacher-librarian introduce one type of information source available in the LMC, for example, the online periodical indexes. After her explanation on how to find the right one to use and on how to actually use the index, that day students are limited to only using

NOVEMBER

Sunday	Monday	Tuesday	Wednesday	Thursday	Friday	Saturday
1	2	3	4	5	6	7
8	9 KWL about topic	10 Develop list of questions about topic that you want answered	11 Create key word list for topic	12 Packet discussion and respon-sibilities	13	14
15	16 **Proposal due** LMC to research -- reference	17 LMC to research -- periodicals	18 LMC to research -- books	19 LMC to research -- Internet	20 LMC to research --	21 Work on Final Drafts of Exit Slips
22	23 Organize Notes. Determine 3-4 main areas (topic sentences)	24 Work on Draft of answers in paragraph form using transitions	25 Organize biblio-graphical information	26 No school	27 No school	28
29	30 Putting it all together				December 4 **Due date for the Paper!!**	

Fig. 7.1. A calendar for a sixth grade I-search assignment.

these periodical indexes for their research—no Internet, no videos. The teacher and teacher-librarian make sure that the students all have an opportunity to find information in an online periodical index. The next day they may move on to specialized encyclopedias, the online catalog, the Internet, or some other information source and spend the day using their newly acquired information skills with each one.

Although the Internet is still the first and most popular place for students to head to for information, I make sure that the students become critical users of the information they find on the Internet before they spend a lot of time searching for sketchy or incorrect information. I know many schools are teaching important Internet skills as part of a technology curriculum. If you are confident that your students know how to use the Internet properly, know how to evaluate websites, and have the information skills necessary to find reliable information quickly by using the Internet, you may allow Internet use from the get-go. Unfortunately, our district does not have this curriculum, so I make sure that time is allowed to teach students how to use the Internet efficiently and how to evaluate websites to make sure the information that students are recording is reliable and accurate. I make sure that this instruction takes place before students can access the Internet. Sometimes this means the Internet is off limits to my students for the first few days of research.

The Illinois Math and Science Academy has a website (http://21cif.imsa.edu) that has tips on teaching Internet fluency to students. For information on teaching students how to evaluate the information found on the Internet, check out the following website: http://www.radcab.com. For lesson plans on teaching critical evaluation of a website, consult http://kathyschrock.net/eval/index.htm.

When you take classes to the school library, do they sit quietly at the library tables, reading through material and diligently taking notes? The stereotypical library where everyone speaks in whispers, careful not to disturb others, is definitely not any middle school library I have been to! I have rarely met an eighth grader who did not consider a trip to the LMC as a social occasion. Why does sitting at those library tables seem to inspire so much conversation, giggling, and frittering away of class time? Because I want to keep socialization to a minimum and maximize actual work, I do not schedule days and days of time in the school library for my students. In fact, scheduling too many days in succession in the school library can be a big waste of time for students. I have learned from experience that the teacher-librarian is the best judge as to how many class periods will be needed for students to gather the needed information in a timely manner. Scheduling the right amount of time cuts down on student socialization and keeps students who are finished with their research from disturbing the others who are in the school library to actually do some work.

After the teacher-librarian has had time to teach my students information literacy skills, and they have checked out their first book, found their first magazine article, or printed out something from the Internet, we are back in the classroom. Students bring this material to the language arts classroom where we spend the class period in a reader's workshop atmosphere. The students seem to be more ready and able to settle down to serious work in the classroom, and I can better monitor what they are doing there as well. This does not mean that the school library is off limits, of course, but I believe that the school library is a place to go for a reason. While it may be a wonderful place to relax, browse, and soak up the literature, research time is precious, and trips to the LMC must be purposeful and efficient. My students are sent there for a purpose. Before I allow a student to leave the classroom for the school library, I talk to him about what he intends to look for. Is he searching for a new book? A magazine article? I encourage students to consult with the teacher-librarian for suggestions on where to look for additional information. I, too, offer suggestions and remind the students to have pen and paper ready to record the information they find. Because they have a purpose in going to the school library, students have cut down on the amount of time they spend procrastinating or just fooling around. Fortunately, the school library is run on a flexible schedule that will accommodate my students whenever they have an information need. If you are not so lucky, be sure to consult with your teacher-librarian for suggestions on how to make your class's scheduled time in the LMC purposeful.

Another way I keep tabs on the progress of my students is to use exit slips. The exit slip is a log kept on one sheet of paper. This slip is collected at the end of each class period or after each research experience in the LMC. I look over the exit slips each night and hand them back to the students the next day. On the slip, students write their answers to three questions.

The first question to be answered on the exit slip is "What did you accomplish today?" I expect students to be specific and avoid a vague answer like "I read some stuff on my topic." I want them to reflect on exactly what they learned or what strategies they employed that day to find new information.

The second question is "What will you do next?" This is a very important question, and one I monitor closely. The answer gives direction to the next day's work, so that there is no reason for floundering around at the beginning of the next class period. It also tells me how the student is progressing.

The final question on the exit slip, "Any questions or concerns?" gives students a chance to tell me how I can help them and gives them an opportunity to express any frustrations they are having with the research process. I can usually answer by adding a note to them on the exit slip—maybe just a simple suggestion about a possible keyword to try or a new source to use.

I skim these exit slips every day, a process that only takes a short time but gives me a handle on where students are and how they are doing. It helps minimize many problems. For example, some students, especially those quiet ones who look industrious but have really accomplished nothing, are less able to slip through the cracks if I can monitor their progress through exit slips. Because the exit slip is one sheet of paper that is added on each day, I can spot quickly if the student is procrastinating or confused. For example, if a student were to write a couple of days in a row, "I am reading an article in *Newsweek.*" "Hmm," I'll wonder, "why hasn't he finished that article yet?" I will make a note to myself to discuss this with the student. Or, if I read, "I am going to look for a new book" after a student has just gone to the school library to check out a book, I may talk to the student and ask, "What was the problem with the book you just checked out? Was it too difficult? Did you actually read it or only skim through it? Does it not answer your questions about the topic?" Often a brief conversation can help me guide the student appropriately.

Teachers who are concerned about whether students are using their allotted library time profitably can use the exit slip idea to keep track of what their students are doing. In fact, it is a good idea to use exit slips every time students visit the school library. If students know they will need to fill out an exit slip at the end of the period, they usually catch on early that it is necessary to use their time wisely and be responsible for what they are doing. The exit slip strategy forces them to be more aware and spend time actually doing some research and taking notes.

Figure 7.2 is a sample of exit slip exchanges I have had with two of my students. I have found that reading and commenting on the exit slips is a very fast process that takes little of my time but pays big dividends. We all know how difficult it can be for teachers to consult with every child in every class period, and the exit slips help me "converse" with everyone, even if it's only to say, "Okay. You're doing great!"

Although the exit slip strategy has worked very well for me, I know that some teachers want students to more fully document the time they have spent researching. They may require students to produce a log describing all the activities they undertook during the course of the research project—what they did, what resources they used to find information, what they found out about their topic. This written record is most often handed in at the end of the assignment, becoming a part of the final project that is assessed. Making this record a part of the paper follows the five-step I-search paper that is described by Ken Macrorie in his book. In his I-search model, students are not only writing up the results of their research, they are also telling how and where they found the information and how they used their time during the research project. Most teachers use this written piece to allow students the opportunity to reflect on their experience and include what the student learned as part of the process—things he did wrong and what he might do differently the next time he is assigned a research project.

> For more information on Macrorie's I-search model and for an example of a student's I-search paper, consult the following website: http://www2.edc.org/FSC/MIH/i-search.html.

During research time students are busy finding sources, reading, taking notes, reviewing their questions, developing new ones, and researching some more. Often students become very enthusiastic, excited, and, yes, opinionated about their topics. They are dying to share what they have learned and also are curious about how their friends are doing. Because I am pleased to see that students are learning and thinking about their topics, I like to give my students opportunities to share their thoughts with the rest of the class before they begin the actual writing of their papers. Occasionally, instead of doing an exit slip at the end of the class period, I begin the class by asking students to write down something new or different they have learned about their topic. I prompt them by asking if there is something that has struck them in some way. I ask what has either surprised them, shocked them, or confused them. I give the students time to write down something that they would like to share with the class, then I give students the opportunity to share this information in a small-group setting. This activity allows time for students to both share their information with others and also learn a little bit about topics other than their own. A sharing day like this provides a time-out from the sometimes tedious routine of researching and note taking and gives the students a feeling of empowerment. They are truly becoming experts on an important issue, and their classmates are looking to them for examples of their newly forming expertise. I point out that while everyone is entitled to an opinion, an educated opinion is a more valuable one. What an "aha!" moment it is for them to refute someone else's perception by rebutting with some statistics or examples. They are reacting with actual facts rather than an emotional, "Well, that's just the way I feel" reaction.

Sometimes I use a thinking log instead of an exit slip at the end of a class period. In the thinking log,

SAMPLE EXIT SLIP

Student:	Today I learned how to use Infotrac. Tomorrow I will use Infotrac and find some articles on gun control for notes. Also look for another book on my topic.
Teacher:	*Sounds like a lot for one day. Focus on finding and reading one or two articles.*
Student:	Today I found a good article about gun control. I printed it off so I can read it and take notes. Tomorrow I will try to find another article.
Teacher:	*Great plan! Keep reading.*
Student:	Today I found another article. I printed it off, I started reading it but I don't get it.
Teacher:	*Show me the article or see me about how to find articles that you will be able to understand. Some of the sources in Infotrac are pretty difficult to read.*
Student:	I took notes on the new article I found.
Teacher:	*Keep reading, and let me know if you need any more help.*

Fig. 7.2.   A sample of exit slip exchanges.

students write a thought or an idea that has occurred to them during their research. Like the exit slip, these thinking logs are collected, read, and handed back to the students the next day. Thinking logs demonstrate to me that a student is engaged in the research process and contemplating the information that he has discovered about the topic he has chosen to research. For example, a student who wonders why so many more girls than boys are afflicted with eating disorders might record something to that effect in her thinking log. After reading this comment, I may reply by asking her if she felt the media might contribute to girls' feelings about body image. This little nudge could push her into further research on exploring how the portrayal of girls in the media might affect this disorder. Another comment I have often seen in thinking logs of those students who are exploring the death penalty is "I used to be for the death penalty, but now I am not so sure. I'm confused, because there are good points on each side." This kind of remark shows me that the researcher is looking at multiple aspects of the issue with an open mind. Figure 7.3 gives further examples of entries in a thinking log, along with my teacher comments.

I am delighted to encourage confused and frustrated students by commenting to them that the confusion shows that they are learning to examine the issue in an open-minded way. This is heady stuff for eighth graders! After all, if there were really only one obvious way to solve a problem, there would be no controversy. Ex-changes via an exit slip or a thinking log, collected and responded to every day, help me keep track of kids and keep kids on track! It assures me that some actual work is being done, and students are not waiting until the last minute to actually concentrate on the project.

FURTHER READING

For more information on the I-search model, consult the following books:

Duncan, Donna, and Laura Lockhart. *I-Search for Success.* New York: Neal Schuman, 2005.

Duncan, Donna, and Laura Lockhart. *I Search, You Search, We All Learn to Research.* New York: Neal Schuman, 2000.

Jent, Amy. My I-piphany. *Knowledge Quest* (March–April 2004): 32–35.

Macrorie, Ken. *The I-Search Paper: Revised Edition of Teaching Writing.* Portsmouth, NH: Boynton/Cook, 1988.

For more information on handouts for every step of the research process, consult the following:

Duncan, Donna, and Laura Lockhart. *I Search, You Search, We All Learn to Research.* New York: Neal Schuman, 2000.

Rankin, Virginia. *The Thoughtful Researcher.* Englewood, CO: Libraries Unlimited, 1999.

Ryan, Jenny. *Information Literacy Toolkit: Grades 7 and Up.* Chicago: ALA, 2001.

Stanley, Deborah B. *Practical Steps to the Research Process for Elementary School.* Englewood, CO: Libraries Unlimited, 2001.

Sample 1

I have learned a lot about bulimia. Something that interested me was that bulimia can affect someone's feelings like they can get angry, frightened, depressed, isolated and lonely a lot. Another thing that interested me was that 9 out of 10 people who get bulimia are females. Males also develop bulimia but not as many as females. I was surprised at that because I didn't know males ever got bulimia.

Teacher response: *Why do you think more females than males are bulimic? See if you can find any reasons for this.*

Sample 2

Something that angers me is some people just start shooting at random. They don't care about anything. Something that confused me about the whole topic of gun control is I understand the second amendment but I also think that it is wrong to just shoot people. I don't know whether to be for gun control or against it.

Teacher response: *It's okay to have mixed feelings. That means you are open-minded. With our freedom to own guns, we pay a high price in deaths. Keep getting reasons to support both sides.*

Sample 3

Today I took a lot of notes on parental notification laws. These laws require teens to tell their parents if they are pregnant and want an abortion. They also need parental consent. I think the reasons behind these laws make sense most of the time. Then teens can get emotional support from their parents. But what if the girls are abused or have troubled family lives? Then they may not want to tell their parents. I think there should be a way around this.

Teacher response: You are really looking at the ramifications of this law! When you consider what can happen to individuals when a law passes, you are really doing some critical thinking!

Fig. 7.3. Further examples of entries in a thinking log, along with my teacher comments.

8

Where's That Green Book I Used Yesterday?

One of the biggest challenges for my middle school students is managing the information they have found while researching their topic. Do you have your students take research notes on 3"-×-5" index cards? Do they ever leave them on the library table? Misplace a few here or there? Forget to write down where they found the information? Do they cram each notecard with long, incomprehensible sentences copied from a source? Or do they print stacks of articles and then slather almost every word on the printout with yellow highlighter? A solution I have found that helps to eliminate some of these problems and also helps to keep them organized is to use notecard sheets and bibliography sheets that can be copied on regular 8"-×-11" paper rather than using the 3"-×-5" index cards. I keep a quantity of these notecards and bibliography sheets in the classroom, and the teacher-librarian always has these sheets available for students in the school library. Since I switched to using these sheets of paper rather than index cards, I have found they make all the difference in the world when it comes to keeping the students' information organized and ready.

An important lesson for students to learn is the necessity to cite sources and how to do this using a recognized format. However, it is easy for teens to forget to record this information while they actually have the source in their hands and before they return it to wherever they found it in the library. Soon a panicky eighth grader is standing at the library counter asking if someone can help him find "the green book that I used last week."

I have trained my students to enter the necessary information about each source on a bibliography sheet before they forget and have returned the resource or have moved on to another source of information. Because the bibliography sheet is a simple way to record information about each source, recording the information just takes each student a second to complete. Figure 8.1 is an example of the bibliography sheet I use in my classroom. It has blanks for students to fill in the infor-

mation about any source they use during their research, whether it is a book, magazine, or website.

Filling in this form serves two important purposes. First, if the student needs to find the source again, he has the source recorded on his bibliography sheet. The student need only find the magazine, encyclopedia volume, or Internet website that he has recorded to return to the information he has found. Books are now easy for the student to find again. Typing the title of a book into the online catalog can lead the student back to the shelf where the book is located. Finding the website or periodical is just as easy. Second, the information on the bibliography sheet can later be used to create a bibliography for the project. When a bibliographic style sheet like the one in figure 8.2 accompanies the bibliography sheet, the student can see what he needs to record and simply fill in the blanks on the bibliography sheet that correspond to the information needed for the citation. Later on, the entries on the bibliography sheet can be formulated into an acceptable bibliography that can be turned in with the assignment.

> For information on how to properly cite information sources or for a bibliography template that students can use for making bibliographic citations, consult the following websites: http://www.noodletools.com or http://www.easybib.com.

Since our school began using these bibliography sheets, some teachers simply require that the students turn in a filled-in bibliography sheet rather than a formal bibliography when they assign research activities. Perusing the bibliography sheets can verify that the student has used several sources for a project.

One of the best things about the bibliography sheet is that each entry has a spot for a number by each recorded source. These numbers are important because they can be tied to notecard sheets. An example of a notecard sheet is provided in figure 8.3. This is the notecard sheet

BIBLIOGRAPHY SHEET

Name _____ Team_____

#____ (Check source type)   ENCYCLOPEDIA ____ VOL. # ____ PERIODICAL ____   BOOK ____

INTERVIEW____   VIDEOTAPE____ PAMPHLET____ INDEX____ INTERNET____

DVD ____   CD-ROM ____ OTHER ____ (identify) _____

TITLE_____

AUTHOR_____PAGES USED _____

TITLE OF ARTICLE_____

PUBLISHER_____ PLACE PUBLISHED _____

DATE PUBLISHED_____ URL_____

#____ (Check source type)   ENCYCLOPEDIA ____ VOL. # ____ PERIODICAL ____   BOOK ____

INTERVIEW____   VIDEOTAPE____ PAMPHLET____ INDEX____ INTERNET____

DVD ____   CD-ROM ____ OTHER ____ (identify) _____

TITLE_____

AUTHOR_____PAGES USED _____

TITLE OF ARTICLE_____

PUBLISHER_____ PLACE PUBLISHED _____

DATE PUBLISHED_____ URL_____

#____ (Check source type)   ENCYCLOPEDIA ____ VOL. # ____ PERIODICAL ____   BOOK ____

INTERVIEW____   VIDEOTAPE____ PAMPHLET____ INDEX____ INTERNET____

DVD ____   CD-ROM ____ OTHER ____ (identify) _____

TITLE_____

AUTHOR_____PAGES USED _____

TITLE OF ARTICLE_____

PUBLISHER_____ PLACE PUBLISHED _____

DATE PUBLISHED_____ URL_____

#____ (Check source type)   ENCYCLOPEDIA ____ VOL. # ____ PERIODICAL ____   BOOK ____

INTERVIEW____   VIDEOTAPE____ PAMPHLET____ INDEX____ INTERNET____

DVD ____   CD-ROM ____ OTHER ____ (identify) _____

TITLE_____

AUTHOR_____PAGES USED _____

TITLE OF ARTICLE_____

PUBLISHER_____ PLACE PUBLISHED _____

DATE PUBLISHED_____ URL_____

Fig. 8.1.   The bibliography sheet I use in my classroom.

BIBLIOGRAPHIC CITATION FORM

Book with One Author:

> Author's last name, Author's first name. <u>Title</u>. Place of publication: Publisher, publication date.

Johnson, Joan. <u>Kids without Homes</u>. New York: Franklin Watts, 1991.

Books with Two Authors:

> First author's last name, First author's first name, and Second author's first name, Second author's last name. <u>Title</u>. Place of publication: Publisher, publication date.

Stavsky, Lois, and J. E. Mozeson. <u>The Place I Call Home</u>. New York: Shapolsky, 1990.

No Author Given:

> <u>Title</u>. Place of Publication: Publisher, publication date.

<u>Homeless in America</u>. Wylie, TX: Information Plus, 1989.

Institution, Association, etc., as Author:

> Institution. <u>Title</u>. Place of publication: Publisher, publication date.

Phi Delta Kappa Educational Foundation. <u>Educating Homeless Children</u>. Bloomington, IN: Phi Delta Kappa, 1990.

Editor as Author:

> Editor's last name, Editor's first name, ed. <u>Title</u>. Place of publication: Publisher, publication date.

Orr, Lisa, ed. <u>The Homeless: Opposing Viewpoints</u>. St. Paul, MN: Greenhaven Press, 1990.

Encyclopedia Article:

> Author's last name, Author's first name. "Title of article," <u>Name of encyclopedia</u>. Year ed.

Hopper, Kim. "Homelessness," <u>World Book Encyclopedia</u>. 1988. (or)

"Homelessness," <u>Academic American Encyclopedia</u>. 1992.

Article in Magazine:

> Author's last name, Author's first name. "Title of article." <u>Name of magazine</u>, Date of magazine, page numbers.

Fig. 8.2. A bibliographic style sheet.

Wells, Amy Stuart. "Educating Homeless Children," <u>Education Digest</u>, April 1990, 30-33.

Pamphlet, Government Document:

| Name of agency. <u>Title of pamphlet,</u> date. |

U. S. House of Representatives. Select Committee on Children, Youth, and Families. <u>The Crisis in Homelessness,</u> 1987.

Software or CD-ROM:

| <u>Title of Software product,</u> date, "Title of article." |

<u>The New Grolier Electronic Encyclopedia,</u> 1992, "Homeless shelters."

Audiovisual Material:

| <u>Title</u> (format), Place of distribution: Distributor, date. |

<u>Life without a Home</u> (video recording), Woodland Hills, CA: Fox Lorber Associates, 1990.

Interview:

| Last name of person interviewed, First name of person interviewed, Organization, Place of interview, Date of interview. |

Freed, Jean, Chicago Homeless Shelter, Chicago, October 15, 1992.

Internet:

| Author. Name of Page. Date of posting/revision. Name of institution/organization affiliated with the site. Date of Access <electronic address> |

DiStefano, Vince. Guidelines for better writing. January 9, 1996.
January 12, 2005 <http://www.usa.net/~vinced/home/better-writing.html/

Online Database:

| Author's name. "Title of article." <u>Name of the online service.</u> Online. Date of access. |

Anderson, John. "Great Depression." Grolier online. Online. November 9, 2004.

Email to You (or other personal communication):

| Author. "Title of message (if any)" E-mail to person's name. Date of message. |

Smith, John. "Re: Gangs." E-mail to the author. November 15, 2004

Fig. 8.2. *Continued*

Name _____ NOTECARDS Team_____

Ref#_____ Page#_____ Ref#_____ Page#_____

☐ quote ☐ quote

Ref#_____ Page#_____ Ref#_____ Page#_____

☐ quote ☐ quote

Ref#_____ Page#_____ Ref#_____ Page#_____

☐ quote ☐ quote

Ref#_____ Page#_____ Ref#_____ Page#_____

☐ quote ☐ quote

Fig. 8.3.   An example of a notecard sheet.

I have my students use to record their notes for my I-search project.

So they know where they got the information that they have written in the square on the notecard sheet, the students are careful to have the numbers on each square of the sheet correspond to the number of the source from which they found the information on the bibliography sheet. Also, the space for notes on the notecard sheets is deliberately small, just big enough to hold one and only one piece of information. This encourages students to summarize information rather than copying word for word from the book, magazine, or website. This also prevents students from recording too much information in each blank—something that occurs quite often when using index cards. If a student records statistics or quotes directly from a source, he only needs to check the quote box in the square where he has recorded this information to know that what is recorded is a "direct quote," and it is necessary for him to give credit to the source in his paper.

Another thing I like about the notecard sheets are their versatility. One variation on the notecard sheets is to fold them vertically, so that students can do double-entry notes. On the left-hand side of the sheet, students can take notes on the important information as usual. On the right hand side of the sheet the researcher can then write reactions, comments, or questions about the information that is recorded on the left-hand side. This format encourages students to do more than mindlessly copy down information. Reading nonfiction is difficult for many students, and requiring double-entry notes encourages students to read actively—to make connections. It prods students to stop and reflect along the way, thinking about what they have read and written down, and giving them a chance to comment on it. Let's say a student is researching the death penalty and has read statistics giving the racial breakdown of those sentenced to death. When the statistics are recorded on the left-hand side of the notecard box, the student may be surprised to see that the number of African Americans is higher than their population numbers would indicate. A comment, written in the right-hand column, "Why is it higher for African Americans?" can provoke further research. Questions are only one kind of comment that can go on the right-hand side. Any reaction or connection along the way can be recorded. These comments, ideas, and opinions of the researcher can easily be successfully incorporated into an I-search paper along with the facts that have been gathered about the topic.

The real beauty to using whole sheets of paper rather than index cards is that each sheet will easily fit into a three-ring binder or folder. Carrying these notes in a three-ring binder is more secure than a bunch of cards with a rubber band around them. Because each bibliography and notecard sheet has a line for the student to

For more information on how to take notes and for lesson plans on teaching students how to take notes, consult the following website: http://www.educationworld.com/a_lesson/lesson/lesson322.shtml. To find additional information and a description of the "trash and treasure" method for teaching note taking, consult the Big 6 website, http://www.big6.com.

record his or her name, lost items are kept to a minimum. While a long-term project may require lots and lots of sheets to be filled in, these notecard sheets are easily transported in a three-ring binder, handy for the student to use when it comes times to write the I-search paper or prepare the PowerPoint presentation.

When students have finished their research and it is time to write the paper, many students may throw up their hands in despair. This is when the beauty of these notecard sheets is revealed. I arm each student with scissors, an envelope (or two) with a hole punched in the corner or side so it can fit in a binder, some paper clips, and sticky notes. Scissors and envelopes? How low-tech! Yes, but the tactile manipulation of working with the notecard sheets engages the brains of students, especially those who thrive with hands-on activities. First, students cut the notecards sheets apart into squares of information. When this is completed, it is time for the students to organize these notes by sorting them into categories. Because the information on the notecards should be the answers to the questions that drove the research, these questions become categories. For example, think about notes that may be recorded about anorexia. Some notes may include a definition of the disorder. Notes on this go in one pile. Any statistics—who has the disorder, how many people afflicted, and so forth—can go into another pile. Another group could include causes and another treatment.

Once the notes are sorted, each pile is paper-clipped together and topped off with a sticky note label identifying the category (subheading). Next, each pile is organized into the order the writer chooses, and there! Outline done! Not on paper with roman numerals, but just paper-clipped piles of notes that can be kept in an envelope. We have spent a lot of effort to make sure the notes have not been lost up to this point. I certainly don't want my students to lose anything now that they have finished taking notes and organizing the notes into a cohesive outline. To ensure the piles of notes are not lost, they are carefully put into a large envelope. To ensure the envelope doesn't get lost, a hole is punched in the top or side, so that it too can be stuck securely in each student's three-ring binder. The envelope is taped shut to make sure the notes stay within it during transportation of the binder.

I believe the simple act of sorting the notecards into piles is the best part of the process. I love watching a classroom full of eighth graders completely engrossed in this task. I can almost hear the brain cells humming with activity as they absorb the information they have written down, determine its importance, and make connections. This is why I do this part of the project in the classroom, rather than having the students do the organization at home. This is also why I continue to use notecard sheets rather than teaching electronic note taking and also because my students do not have the luxury of having computers or laptops at their disposal at all times. Although the method of using notecards is one that has been used for many years, it is still a valuable tool for teaching students to make connections and to teach organization.

The bibliography sheets can be cut apart in the same way as the notecard sheets. When students are equipped with a highlighter and the bibliographic style sheet, they can easily highlight on each entry the word or name that will come first in their bibliographic citation. When everything is highlighted and the bibliography sheet is cut apart, alphabetizing the bibliography is a simple matter.

The teacher-librarian makes sure that notecard and bibliography sheets are available at all times in the library. In fact, during a research assignment, the library staff often has to replenish the supply of notecard sheets several times to accommodate the need for them. Because these sheets are so simple to fill in, and because there is always a supply of them available either in the classroom or the library, there is now no longer any excuse for a student not being able to find a book she had used during her research—unless, of course, it has been checked out! Nobody needs to worry about running out of index cards, and there is no longer any fumbling around to replace rubber bands.

FURTHER READING

For more information on the steps to research and methods for note taking, consult the following sources:

Ballenger, Bruce. *The Curious Researcher: A Guide to Writing Research Papers.* 2nd ed. Boston: Allyn & Bacon, 1998.

Rankin, Virginia. *The Thoughtful Researcher.* Englewood, CO: Libraries Unlimited, 1999.

Stanley, Deborah B. *Practical Steps to the Research Process for High School.* Englewood, CO: Libraries Unlimited, 1999.

Stanley, Deborah B. *Practical Steps to the Research Process for Middle School.* Englewood, CO: Libraries Unlimited, 2000.

9

It's Not Supposed to Be Interesting—It's a Report

The research has been completed, the notes have been organized, and the writer is ready to go! Final projects can take many forms, but I like the tried-and-true I-search paper. How can you help students turn all that newfound information into a cohesive and interesting paper? While writing a comprehensive and thorough paper may be a daunting task for students, breaking the process down into easily managed steps can make the process go much more smoothly.

Figure 9.1 is a sheet that I hand out to students before the actual writing begins. The reason I include this in the research packet that I give my students is because it serves as a guide that students can refer to during the writing of the paper, and it also becomes a checklist for things that students need to be sure to have done upon completion.

Good writing can be created when writers focus on these six essential writing traits: (1) ideas; (2) organization; (3) voice; (4) word choice; (5) sentence fluency; and (6) conventions. By using a clear writing rubric as a tool for teaching expository writing, students have a better understanding of what good writing is and how they can get there. By consistently using a rubric for all my writing assignments, I have discovered that students can gain a true understanding of what makes a good piece of writing because the rubric helps them to know what they can do to create a writing piece that will meet my expectations. I have adapted the rubric designed by Vickie Spandel, author of *Creating Writers through 6-Trait Assessment and Instruction* (2005), to guide writing instruction in my language arts classroom. Spandel's basic rubric can be tweaked by teachers to include specific features of a particular writing genre and adapted to fit most writing assignments. The basic rubric that is detailed in Spandel's book is a tool that I have successfully used for the I-search concerns project and also for all other writing assignments that I assign to students. As you begin to develop your own rubrics, you will realize that you need not assess all six essential writing traits in the written assignment that is turned in by the student. Sometimes I assess organization, word choice, and sentence fluency. Other times I may be more interested in voice and conventions. I change my rubric to reflect what I will be looking at in each assignment. The one constant in any writing assignment, however, is the trait of ideas. It's what the writer has to say—what's informative, new, and interesting to the reader. Ideas are the heart of any piece of writing, and after researching, my students should have lots of ideas to share in their culminating piece.

Before my students begin to write their I-search paper, I have the class check out the rubric that was handed out to them when the I-search project was introduced. In the example rubric in figure 9.2, I have focused on assessing the traits of ideas, organization, voice, and conventions. These are the things that I will be looking for in the students' I-search papers.

How are these traits defined? First of all, what are the keys to a paper strong in ideas? This student-friendly rubric lets the students know that I will be assessing whether the information presented in the paper is accurate and extensive, whether the ideas presented by the author have sufficient support and are illustrated by examples, and whether the author has presented different facets of the issue he is addressing. The rubric lets students know that good organization requires that the paper have a focused and inviting lead, smooth transitions, details that are presented in a logical order, and a strong conclusion that leaves the reader thinking about the topic. The rubric helps students realize that a paper is strong in voice if the writer has put his or her personal, recognizable stamp on it, by demonstrating that the writer cares about the topic and has reflected on his or her findings. The rubric addresses voice by letting writers know that the paper should speak to an audience, encouraging them to consider the writer's

STEPS TO WRITING YOUR I-SEARCH PAPER

ORGANIZE YOUR INFORMATION
1. First, cut apart your notecards.
2. Then, categorize your notecards according to subtopics. For example, you may pile them according to:
   Definition of the issue
   Arguments for
   Arguments against
   Etc.
3. Paper clip each stack of notecards together.
4. Label each stack of notecards according to subtopics with a sticky note.
5. Look through each stack of notecards. Arrange them in the appropriate order.
6. Arrange the stack of notecards in the order that would be appropriate for your paper. For example, put the "Causes of the problem" stack ahead of the "Solutions to the problem" stack.

You have now outlined your information for the body of your paper.
That was easy, wasn't it?

WRITE YOUR INTRODUCTION
1. Read your "Ideas for Leads" handout. Then write a lead that will get the attention of your readers.
2. Include in the introduction to your paper: <u>what</u> your topic is, <u>why</u> you chose to study this topic, and <u>why</u> this is an important topic. Use FIRST PERSON. (For example: "I chose this topic because ……")

WRITE THE BODY OF YOUR PAPER
1. Use transitions to connect your ideas and information. See *Write Source* for a list.
2. Write your information in a clear and logical way.
3. Be sure to put the information in your own voice. (HINT: I can tell the difference when it is copied straight out of a book.) When using direct quotes from a source, identify the source. (For example: According to Joe Schmoe …)
4. Include examples.
5. Include information from any interviews you have conducted.
6. Include your ideas, thoughts, reactions, etc. to the information. You might have sentences like:
   > I wanted to know …
   > I learned …
   > I was surprised …
   > It made me angry to learn …

   Refer to your thinking log for sentences that tell your reactions and feelings.
7. Involve the readers by getting them to think about the topic.
8. When you finish writing about one topic (one stack of notecards), then move on to another set.

(Continued on the back …)

Fig. 9.1.   A sheet that I hand out to students before the actual writing begins.

WRITE A CONCLUSION
1. Sum up what you have learned.
2. Sum up your thoughts and opinions about the topic. Be sure you explain why you feel the way you do.

Now you have finished writing your rough draft!

REVISE YOUR PAPER
1. Read your paper again and determine whether it is clear, logical, interesting, etc.
2. Review the rubric to see how you have done so far with ideas, organization, and voice.
3. Have a critical friend (a teacher, parent, or a friend who can be honest) read your paper and give specific suggestions for making it better.

EDIT YOUR PAPER
1. Check your spelling and punctuation.
2. Get help from a critical friend who knows how to spell.

ORGANIZE YOUR BIBLIOGRAPHY
1. Cut the Bibliography sheet apart.
2. Highlight the author's last name for each source. If no author is given, then highlight the first work in the title of the article, pamphlet, book, etc. (Ignore A, An, or The.)
3. Arrange the bibliographies in alphabetical order.
4. Write the bibliography in the correct form. Refer to the Bibliographic Style Sheet handout or *Write Source* to discover the proper form for each source.

TYPE YOUR FINAL DRAFT
Use a large (12) font. Times New Roman, Arial, or Courier font styles are preferred. Double-space the paper.

CONGRATULATIONS! YOU ARE FINISHED!

Fig. 9.1. *Continued*

RESEARCH PAPER 6-POINT RUBRIC

IDEAS

6

My ideas are crystal clear and focused.

I have insight and an in-depth understanding of my topic.

I have thoughtfully selected researched details that are rich, significant, and accurate.

My details are intriguing – not just things everyone knows.

5

My paper is clear and focused throughout.

I have a strong main idea.

I used research to make my writing convincing and authentic.

My main idea is expanded and well-supported with accurate details and evidence.

I use important details.

4

Most of my paper is clear and focused.

It is easy to tell where this paper is headed.

I have some great details.

I might have some generalities and need to dig deeper.

I need some more information to give a more complete and accurate picture.

3

General information provides the big picture.

I usually stick to my topic.

Some "details" may be things that readers already know.

Some information may be inaccurate.

There might a lot of generalities, clichéd thinking, and filler.

My topic might be too big. I need to "zoom in" more.

2

There is just a hint of a main idea This is pretty sketchy. I didn't say much.

Inaccurate information can confuse the reader.

Factlets or tidbits may not support my main idea.

1

These are just notes and thoughts.

Readers will have to guess at a main idea.

Inaccurate information.

ORGANIZATION

6

My paper has a thoughtful structure that guides the reader through the text. Super organization makes my ideas clear.

The lead is unforgettable. Conclusion is enlightening and leaves the reader thinking.

Transitions are satisfying and well crafted.

5

Order works well with my topic and my purpose.

The structure is evident, but not too obvious.

I have a lead that is interesting and inviting.

My conclusion feels just right.

I have smooth transitions.

4

The order works – readers will not get lost.

My structure is definitely there, but might be a little predictable.

I have a lead and a conclusion that do the job.

My transitions are there and are usually helpful.

3

Some parts may be out of order.

I have a lead and a conclusion, but one or both of them may need work.

Transitions may be unclear or may be too obvious and predictable.

It might be hard to see how some of my ideas are connected.

2

Hard to follow! I seem to go in different directions.

I don't connect ideas to my main point.

Lead and/ or conclusion may be missing or dull.

Transitions are unclear or missing.

1

This is just a jumble of details and random thoughts.

Nothing goes with anything else.

There is no lead. It just begins.

There is not conclusion. It just stops.

VOICE

6

This is ME! It's as individual as my fingerprints.

This paper begs to be read aloud. You want to share it.

I love this topic! I don't overwrite, but I use my voice to keep readers hooked.

My tone and flavor enhance my topic and purpose.

A reader will find this paper tough to put down.

5

My voice is lively, expressive, and enthusiastic.

The tone and flavor are right for my topic, audience, and purpose.

I want my audience to like this topic and to tune in, and it shows in my writing.

4

I show some sparks of individuality, enthusiasm, and spontaneity.

Tone and flavor are acceptable for topic, audience, and purpose.

I have some strong moments, but my voice comes and goes.

My paper may not be unique.

3

My writing is sincere. This sounds like an OK paper.

My tone may not be a perfect fit for the audience, topic, or purpose.

I seem distant from my audience.

I don't think about my audience. I just write.

2

Sometimes I may sound like an encyclopedia.

Sometimes I may sound too chatty.

Tone and flavor are inappropriate.

I don't sound like I care too much about what I am writing.

I don't care about my audience too much.

1

Voice is missing from this paper.

It does not sound like an individual wrote this paper.

If I liked this topic or knew more about it, I could put more into it.

The reader will probably be bored.

CONVENTIONS

6

Only the pickiest of editors will spot errors.

I have shown that I have mastered a wide variety of conventions.

I have correctly cited sources.

The layout is enticing.

5

Any minor errors are easily overlooked.

I did proofread carefully and it shows.

I used good conventions to make my text easy to read.

I have correctly cited sources.

There is sufficient length and complexity to demonstrate a range of conventions appropriate to the writer's grade level.

The layout is appropriate.

4

I made some noticeable but minor errors.

It is readable but lacks close attention to editing.

A more thorough once-over is needed before publication.

Sources may not be cited accurately.

Basics are OK.

Layout is acceptable.

3

There are a few noticeable, distracting errors.

There are some errors on some basics, like periods and spelling.

Errors occur in bibliographical citations.

There may be some run-on sentences, comma splices, or errors in usage, grammar or verb tense.

Thorough editing is needed.

Layout may need some attention.

2

This has many errors.

Some errors get in the way of meaning.

Line-by-line editing is needed.

Limited attention has been given to layout.

Citations are inaccurate or missing.

1

Serious frequent errors make reading this extremely difficult.

I need some help with editing.

Citations are missing.

Fig. 9.2. A rubric that focuses on assessing the traits of ideas, organization, voice, and conventions.

position on the issue. During the editing process, I expect students to focus on preparing a paper that is free of grammatical and spelling errors with proper punctuation evident, thus addressing the trait of conventions. This rubric example lets students know that I will be looking for ideas, organization, voice, and conventions as I assess the papers that have been submitted. By giving the rubric ahead of the actual writing, students will have no confusion about how I will be assessing their project at the end of the assignment.

Organizing lots of information seems to be the biggest obstacle for young writers when it comes to creating good research papers. Even while they are gathering their facts, students often approach me with the question "How am I going to put all of this together?" I assure skeptical students that it will work out just fine. The process of cutting and sorting the notecards, analyzing the information written on each notecard, and then deciding which category it belongs in demonstrates to the students that the organization of lots of information can be done after all! An outline may help the writer put his information into logical order, but haven't some of us been guilty of writing an outline after the paper is written instead of before? Then what's the point? A formal outline is not the only or even the best way to organize information, so other simpler and more effective ways should be taught. Organizing the notecards into piles is a much simpler activity that teaches students how to organize their research. This organization of the notecards and the arrangement of the notecards into a logical sequence take the place of writing an actual outline. Actual writing does not occur until students have finished organizing their notecards into clipped-together stacks, and the stacks are arranged in the order in which the student wants the information to appear in his paper.

While most traditional term papers are written in the third person, I prefer the first person, as modeled in Mackrorie's I-search model. Why? The first-person style best reflects the learning outcomes of the project.

My goal is for students to think critically about their topic, to make connections, to analyze information, and to draw conclusions. The first-person format gives the writer a vehicle for expressing his or her ideas on the issue, rather than simply regurgitating the facts that have been gathered. First person allows the voice of the writer to interject his own opinions into the piece. Many students have chosen to learn about a topic that is highly controversial—capital punishment, gun control, violence in the media, peer pressure. They have formed opinions on these issues. An I-search paper gives them an opportunity to not only report some facts but to also take a stance on an issue. It encourages the writer to consider word choice and sentence style—traits of engaging writing that are sometimes left out of the deadly dull third-person reports that are usually assigned.

Haven't you been put to sleep by lifeless prose? On the other hand, haven't you been engrossed by a compelling description of actual events or an illuminating explanation? A strong and engaging voice is not only an element of good fiction but of nonfiction as well. Throughout the school year, well before we tackle writing our I-search papers, we read, enjoy, and examine various examples of nonfiction writing found in magazines, newspapers, on websites, or on blogs that demonstrate that nonfiction can have a lively and engaging voice as well as "just the facts." The voice of a writer is always important and cannot be put aside when research reports are written. By requiring that the piece be written in the first person, the paper becomes more interesting to write and, of course, to read. Good I-search papers almost invite the reader to jump into the text himself.

A final reason why I prefer the first-person format is that it is an additional safeguard against plagiarism. Although plagiarism is addressed in depth in the next chapter, it is important to note that because students are expected to react to the information in a personal way rather than to just report it, copying a piece from the Internet is more difficult, because most of the papers published on the Internet are written in third-person.

> Further information on teaching the I-search process can be found at http://www.literacymatters.org/content/isearch/intro.htm or http://www2.edc.org/FSC/MIH/i-search.html.

A good lead is important to any written exercise, and I have created a mini-lesson on effective leads to get the creative juices flowing in my students. I tell them that there are many more ways to begin their writing than the trite statement "My report is on the death penalty." We look at some of the books or articles that the students have been reading and discuss the ways real writers begin their pieces. Figure 9.3 is a handout that I give to my students that gives them several options for effective lead paragraphs that will immediately engage the reader.

After introducing several options and discussing them, I encourage students to write two or three possible leads, and then choose one that they feel is a real "grabber."

After the students have an idea for an effective lead for their paper, we discuss the promise statement, also known as a thesis statement. This statement promises the reader that the paper will have a focus. It gives direction to the piece by providing the writer with a purpose for writing the paper. I ask my students, "Why

IDEAS FOR LEADS

Typical lead

My report is about the forests in the American Northwest. This topic is an important one because there is a lot of controversy surrounding the rights of the loggers versus the protection of the endangered species, the spotted owl.

Speak to the reader

Begin your lead with a statement that puts your reader into the subject.

Imagine that you are a logger in the American Northwest. You have always earned your living in the lumber industry. Your friends and family in your town also have been employed in the lumber industry for many years, even generations. Now your source of income is being threatened by those who wish to protect the spotted owl.

Other opening could be:
Picture this …
You might think that _____, but _____
Can you imagine ….?

Question lead

Ask your reader a question to get them thinking about the topic.
Have you ever wondered … ?
What do you think … ?
Can you imagine … ?
Did you know that … ?

Surprising fact

Begin your paper with a surprising or startling fact about your topic.

In the state of Oregon, twenty percent of the population is employed by the logging industry. Can you imagine all of the problems that could arise if the cutting down of trees would suddenly be banned in the state? This paper will take a look at this controversial issue.

Descriptive or Action lead

Set the scene with a description of a person, place thing or event that relates to your topic. Then follow this description with an explanation of why this is the subject of your research.

The shabbily dressed old woman dragged a rusted old shopping cart down the street. The cart was filled with ripped, dirty trash bags that spewed the woman's possessions. As she trudged along, she stopped at each trash can on the street, and rummaged through its contents. Occasionally she retrieved something from a can an added it to the possessions she had in her cart.

Quotation lead

Choose a quotation from another source that has made an impact on you. Begin your paper with this quotation. A quotation can be from a famous person, from a person involved in your topic (for example; a homeless person), or from a poem or another piece of literature.
Poor is a tired face.
Poor is thin.
Poor is standing outside
Looking in.
      -- Myra Cohn Livingston   (BE SURE TO GIVE CREDIT TO AUTHORS.)

Feelings lead

A feelings lead expresses your feelings on a topic.

I first became interested in the plight of the homeless when my family and I visited Washington, D.C. While we were having lunch at an outdoor food stand, we noticed a dirty unshaven man rummaging through the trash in search of discarded hamburgers or fries to eat.

Fig. 9.3. A handout that shows several options for effective lead paragraphs that will immediately engage the reader.

is this topic so important to you? What do you want to tell your readers about it? What do you want the reader to know after reading your paper?" This helps them to focus on the promise statement for the paper. A sentence or paragraph that includes the promise statement usually comes after the lead paragraph and before the students begin the actual discussion of what they have found out about their topic.

Once the lead paragraph and the promise statement are written, students can begin the actual writing of the paper. The notecards that they have sorted will become the "heart" of the paper. Beginning with the first stack of notecards, students reexamine their facts, determining what information they want to include in the first paragraph and in what order. It is a pleasure to observe how confidence builds when students have the lead paragraph, promise statement, and first paragraph under their belts.

The students will have to make many decisions during their writing, pondering the following questions: Will I paraphrase the information or use exact quotes? How can I make the language understandable to someone who knows nothing about this topic? Will I need examples to enhance understanding? The teacher serves as coach, guide, and consultant, available to confer with students as necessary and to help them answer these important questions.

When a student has completed writing about one stack of notecards, he simply moves on to the next, then the next, and so on. Students often express amazement at how simple this process is, finding that the paper is almost writing itself because of the preliminary work of researching and, especially, organizing the information into categories. The writers are on a roll, and now it just takes time to complete the paper. Once all the notecards are dispensed with, the paper needs only a conclusion to complete the rough draft.

The notecard piles also keep that nemesis—procrastination—at bay! Who hasn't burned the midnight oil, sitting bleary-eyed over a paper left until the last minute? Although we may have learned the hard way that setting deadlines along the way is really the way to go, it is hard to instill this time management into students. This is especially hard when students can have varying amounts of material to write about. Some students may have 500 notecards, while others have only 200. To make sure my students don't procrastinate, I simply assign them percents. For example, for a paper that is due in two weeks, I give them guidelines by stating that by Tuesday they need to have 25 percent of the notecards used; by Friday, 50 percent must be completed; and so on. Students react favorably to this method. The notecard stacks are a tangible way to see how much has been done and how much is left to be written. This prevents

that false sense of "This won't take long" that can trip up writers and encourage procrastination.

Personal comments can be included in the I-search paper. In fact, they are encouraged! Both the thinking logs, mentioned before, and double-entry note taking are research tools that invite students to ask questions, make connections, and synthesize information before the actual writing takes place. These comments can provide students with a brief history of their thinking and can be a valuable addition to their papers. As the students revisit their thinking logs and review any comments written on their notes, they are able to include these insights into their actual papers. These personal insights make the paper the writer's own.

> Students can find additional information and links to websites that will help them in the actual writing of the paper at http://www.ipl.org/div/aplus/linkswritingstyle.htm.

Before they know it, the papers are written, and my students are amazed at how the notecard sheets and the thinking logs have been instrumental in making the process go smoothly. Just like building a house, if you have the right tools at your disposal, things are a lot easier. My students have learned that taking good notes and reflecting on what they have found makes writing the paper much easier and more interesting to write.

An important part of the writing process is revision. After revisiting the rubric, students are able to evaluate their papers with a critical eye, underlining or highlighting any traits on the rubric that apply to their paper. This helps them to identify qualities that need improvement. Recognizing where improvement is needed helps students in the revision process.

The editing of the paper is important in order to achieve an error-free final draft. Mini-lessons on punctuation pitfalls and paragraphing, as well as encouraging the use of spell checkers are ways to keep some of these grammatical mistakes from the final draft. I also suggest that the students read their papers aloud because this often helps with the writing and revising. Doing these simple tasks enables students to make the paper free of grammatical errors, thus understanding what is meant in the rubric regarding conventions.

It is never too early to teach academic integrity, and students of any age need to understand the importance of giving credit to sources. Each teacher has his own requirement for how quotes within the paper are to be handled. It is important that students learn what needs to be acknowledged and how to cite the source when acknowledging something that is not their own. Although I tend to be more lenient with eighth graders, probably because I do require that they submit a bibliography detailing all the sources they used in gathering information for the paper, it is important for students to learn to give credit to others for their work.

Preparing the bibliography can be a nightmare of misplaced essentials, such as the author and publisher, but the use of the bibliography sheets described in chapter 8 can come to the rescue. When students are taught to properly fill in the spaces on the bibliography sheet whenever a new source is used, the necessary information is available for the bibliographic citation. Using the bibliography sheet should prevent those last-minute trips to the school library to search for the copyright date of a book or the page number of the magazine article. Models of correctly cited samples can guide students to the correct format for the bibliography. No matter what style sheet or manual is used, the important thing is that an example is given for every type of source, including websites and online sources, which are heavily used by the techno-savvy researchers of today.

Just as they did with the notecard sheets, students cut apart the bibliography sheets. But first, I ask them to highlight the author or other word that will come first in the bibliographic citation. Then when the sheets are cut apart, they can be alphabetized easily, creating the proper bibliography.

When the papers are completed, I remind students of the long papers that they read from previous students before we began the project, by saying, "Remember when you thought you couldn't possibly write a paper this complicated or this long? Well, you have!" The completion of this long process is definitely something to celebrate!

These papers deserve an audience! Eighth graders are often reticent about showing their work to a parent, but at the same time they bask in the praise that parents bestow on them for a job well done. As part of the assignment, students need to return an adult comment form (figure 9.4) to accompany the final draft on its due date.

This form invites an adult to read the paper and comment on it. I tell students that the adult who reads the paper does not necessarily have to be a parent. It could also be a favorite teacher. In any case, when I have read these completed forms, I find that most adults chosen by the students include an effusive, complimentary comment about the paper. What writer wouldn't be encouraged when he is complimented on his work? Having an adult help the students in this way sets a great precedent for future writing experiences. It is also a way for students to get their parents involved in the research experience. How many parents have actually ever read the papers their students have submitted? My guess is "not many." This is a way to get the parents involved in the research process and writing but not doing the actual work for their child.

Peer conferences are an effective method to improve the quality of the finished product, as long as the conferences center on the traits of a good piece of writing. Figure 9.5 is an effective tool I have used to help students with peer conferences.

Students are paired with a partner, and after exchanging rough drafts, they are given a copy of this evaluation form. The form helps students focus on the important things in the paper. Specific feedback such as "I don't understand this sentence," "Can you include an example here?" or "Why did you say you agreed with this idea?" can direct the writer to constructive ways to enhance the paper. Besides helping each other improve their papers, students get to learn new things about writing and about their partner's topic!

In spite of their protestations to the contrary, students enjoy sharing their work with each other, and there are a number of ways to orchestrate this in addition to the peer conference. Reading papers in front of the class can be deadly dull and also a dreaded experience for teens, so I avoid these. Forming small conversational groups where students can read excerpts of their papers and discuss the issues is much less threatening and engaging. I also have invited feedback from peers by handing out papers at random and asking students to read the one he was given and write one comment about it. Then the student takes another paper and does the same, until time runs out for this activity. Contrary to what you may think, students like reading what others have written, as well as seeing how others have reacted to their written pieces. At the end of the class, we spend a few minutes answering the question, "Who read something good today?" Students beam when classmates not only single out their writing but also explain the traits that made it a good paper. What excellent reinforcement for doing the "write" thing!

The final step before the I-search papers are collected is for the students to reflect on the entire research experience. Students usually are pleased by their efforts, but I try to get them to see the purpose in the assignment. How did they grow in their research and writing skills? A self-assessment allows them to see how they have developed in confidence because of the experience. An added advantage to having students reflect on the research experience is that these self-assessment opportunities also give me insight as to how I can improve the project for future classes. The self-assessment form in figure 9.6 asks

Dear _____ ,

This quarter I have been working on a research project, and I have completed my I-Search paper. A good I-Search paper should:

- be well-researched, thorough, and accurate;
- include different points of view;
- be well-organized;
- show that the writer understands the topic;
- expresses the writer's thoughts and ideas about the topic;
- have an attention-getting lead and variety of sentence types;
- be free of spelling and punctuation errors;
- include a bibliography;
- and engage the reader.

Please read my paper and write a comment about it. Thanks!

Reader's comments:

_____

_____

_____

_____

_____

_____

_____

_____

Fig. 9.4. An adult comment form.

CONCERNS PAPER PARTNER CONFERENCE

Name of author_____

Name of partner _____

1. Does the lead grab your attention?   Y   N

2. Does the lead show why the topic is important?   Y   N

3. Does the intro tell what the paper is about?   Y   N

4. How could the intro be improved?

_____

_____

5. Does each section of the body begin with a topic sentence?   Y   N

6. Are there transitions to connect one section to another?   Y   N

7. Can you, the reader, understand everything in the paper?   Y   N

8. Does the writer give credit when sources are quoted?   Y   N

9. Does the writer sound like he/ she is talking to the reader? Y   N

10. Does the writer include his/ her opinions, feelings, etc.?   Y   N

11. Does the writer support his/ her opinions with reasons?   Y   N

!2. What parts could be clearer and easier to understand?

_____

_____

13. Where can the writer add more opinions, feelings, etc.?

_____

_____

 14. What else can the writer do to make the body of the paper better?

_____

_____

15. Does the conclusion sum up the information in the paper?   Y   N

16. Does the writer sum up his/ her ideas about the topic?   Y   N

********** *On the back, write a comment about what you think is the best part of this paper. Then make suggestions about what the author can do to improve the paper.*

Fig. 9.5.   An effective tool to help students with peer conferences.

I-SEARCH SELF ASSESSMENT

What strategies did you learn and what strategies did you use while researching and writing this paper? Consider strategies in each of the following categories:

Thinking skills _____
_____
_____
_____

Research skills _____
_____
_____
_____

Organizational skills _____
_____
_____
_____

Writing skills _____
_____
_____

Do you believe this to be a worthwhile project? Why or why not? _____
_____
_____

What did you *like* about this project? Why? _____
_____
_____

What did you *dislike*? Why? _____
_____
_____

What are some things that Mrs. Brosnahan did that were *helpful* to you as you worked on this project? _____
_____
_____

What are some things that Mrs. Brosnahan *could have done* to help you on this project? _____
_____
_____

Fig. 9.6.   A self-assessment form.

students to look critically at the research project, and it gives students an opportunity to give me feedback on the assignment. Students are very honest, and surprisingly, I have used many of their comments to "tweak" the assignment over the years.

FURTHER READING

For more information on the actual writing of a research paper, consult the following:

California School Library Association. *From Library Skills to Information Literacy: A Handbook for the 21st Century*. 2nd ed. San Jose, CA: Hi-Willow Research, 1997.

Duncan, Donna, and Laura Lockhart. *I Search, You Search, We All Learn to Research*. New York: Neal Schuman, 2000.

Joyce, Marilyn, and Julie I. Tallman. *Making the Writing and Research Connection with the I-Search Process: A How-to-Do-It Manual*. New York: Neal-Schuman, 1987.

Mackrorie, Ken. *The I-Search Paper: Revised Edition of Searching Writing*. Portsmouth, NH: Boynton Cook, 1988.

Spandel, Vicki. *Creating Writers through 6-Trait Assessment and Instruction*. 4th ed. Upper Saddle River, NJ: Pearson Education, 2005.

10

I'll Just Copy It off the Internet

Plagiarism has reared its ugly head in academia and the publishing world for ages. In recent years, we have seen the issue of plagiarism splashed on the pages of news magazines and supermarket periodicals, and leading off the prime-time news. In fact, ABC has even broadcast an hour-long news special that addressed how today's high school and college students are using new technology to help them cheat on everything from tests to research reports. Just as the "Information Age" has made it easier to find information on just about any topic, it has also made it easier for students to cheat and plagiarize.

For examples of plagiarism in the news and links to plagiarism resources, consult the following website: http://www .plagiarized.com.

With plenty of bad examples of cheating, how can we ensure that our students will work with integrity? Fully aware that students can often be tempted to copy whole sections of information off the Internet or out of books, I use the following strategies to dissuade students from being tempted to plagiarize or take credit for work that is not theirs.

First of all, let's think about why students might plagiarize. One reason seems to be that students don't really understand what plagiarizing is. I begin in the classroom with a discussion of plagiarism. My talk comes as students are beginning the research for their project, shortly after the assignment is given rather than after students have already begun the project. In my presentation, I talk about what it means to plagiarize and mention the possible consequences when plagiarism is found. I find it helpful to show students examples of plagiarism from real life. Your teacher librarian may also be able to find examples of plagiarism to share with your class. I give students time to discuss what their reactions would be if someone else took credit for their work and to express their feelings about Internet

You can visit the following website for links to PowerPoint presentations on plagiarism: http://www.teacherlibrarian.com/tltoolkit/web_wonders/wonders_30_1.html. An online plagiarism tutorial to use with students can be found at http://library .acadiau.ca/tutorials/plagiarism. Students can consult the following website for the Student Guide to Plagiarism: http://www.education-world.com/a_curr/TM/curr390_guide.shtml.

sites that sell research papers. Students do have a good sense of right and wrong. A mini-lesson on plagiarism not only clarifies what plagiarism is for the students, it also gives me an opportunity to let them know that I will be on the lookout for it.

Many schools also have policies in place that detail the penalties for students who are caught plagiarizing. The policy may put a student who is found plagiarizing in the same category as someone who is caught cheating on a test. These policies are usually spelled out in student handbooks that are given to everyone at the beginning of the school year. Often punishments can be quite severe—being given a zero for the assignment or suspension from school, for example. If your school has one of these policies in place, it might be advantageous to revisit the student handbook at the beginning of the research project to remind students that plagiarism is taken very seriously in your school and to make students aware of how carefully you will be looking for any evidence of plagiarism in their projects.

A template that can be used for writing a plagiarism policy can be found at http://www.noodletools.com/debbie/ethical/.

In addition to realizing the moral implications to plagiarizing a part of their papers or copying a complete paper from an online source and taking credit for it, I create a climate in my class that de-emphasizes grades and accentuates learning. While the quest for an A can overshadow learning, I use other methods to get students engaged in the research process. The question "What do you want to know?" is the heart of the I-search process and the key to the start of learning. When students have a choice in deciding on the topic that they want to explore, I know that the desire to learn more about something in which they are interested makes it less likely for students to plagiarize sections of their assignment or to copy an entire paper. When delving into a topic of our own choice, we are curious and eager to answer our own questions. We wouldn't dream of mindlessly copying facts from a book or an encyclopedia because we would recognize that we weren't learning. The best assignments, then, come from a student's own interests. Although I do give students suggestions of topics they might want to consider, I do not mandate that they research a specific topic. Allowing students choices among several topics gives them the freedom to choose one in which they have an interest and is one that they want to pursue. Usually my students can find something to research that interests them. If not, I am open to student suggestions of topics that are not included in my suggested topic list.

Sometimes students choose to plagiarize because they do not have the essential research skills necessary to complete the project or they procrastinate and then panic when a deadline looms. These issues are, of course, what this entire book addresses. Research is not assigned; it's taught. When we guide students through the research process, confirming along the way that they can be successful, they won't feel the need to copy the work of others. The I-search project that I do with my eighth graders isn't simply "assigned," it is "taught." I remember back when I was in school. Then teachers simply assigned a term paper and told us when it was due. I showed up on that day toting my finished project. Back then, the teacher assumed that I knew all the steps to research, including how to find information, take notes, organize and write the paper, and cite sources. It might have taken some personal learning on my part, but somehow I complied. I now know that when I simply assign a research project and give my students a due date but do not give them the instruction they need and deserve to complete a quality project, I am setting them up for failure. When a research project is assigned without knowing if students have the requisite skills to complete it successfully, a desperate student may use any means at his disposal to complete the assignment, including copying a paper that another student has used or buying a paper from one of the sites on the Internet.

Because I am not assigning research papers but teaching the research process, I am monitoring my students' work on a daily basis. When I emphasize the process, this means I am involved in every step of the project—the topic proposal, the note taking, the writing of multiple drafts, the working bibliography. I also make sure to allow enough time to monitor progress and give my students the instruction and help they need to be successful. I don't simply assign the project and let the kids loose and then collect the papers a few weeks later. My I-search project requires extensive research that takes place over a four- to six-week span. During those weeks, I am constantly monitoring my students' progress by allowing class time for the project, using exit slips and thinking logs, and being available to help students along the way. It would be next to impossible for students to "fake" this when I am keeping such close watch on what is happening. I suppose kids could fool me, but who would want to go to all the trouble of pretense?

Additionally, if I am only asking students to regurgitate facts, a savvy student will figure out right away that all he needs to do is to copy stuff out of an encyclopedia. What a waste of time for everyone! A valuable assignment requires students to process information, to apply it to new situations, and to synthesize and evaluate ideas. This means that I must structure any research assignment so that it is impossible for students to simply copy facts. For instance, it is easy for students to find information on Al-Qaeda. But if the assignment asks them to discuss solutions to terrorism, students need to evaluate information and draw their own conclusions about what can be done to stem the effects of terrorism across the globe. Assignments that force students to compare, contrast, or synthesize the information that they collect are far less likely to be plagiarized.

> To read articles on how to structure assignments that alleviate the possibility of plagiarism, consult the following websites: http://www.doug-johnson.com/dougwri/plagiarism-proofing-assignments.html and http://www.fno.org/may98/cov98may.html.

I make sure that students also learn the proper way to give sources credit for the information they use in their papers. I spend time making sure that students know how to cite quotes and statistics in their papers. I spend time teaching students the proper techniques to paraphrase and provide them with instruction in how to construct the bibliography that will be part of the I-search project. Teaching students the proper methods for using information from many different sources and making sure that they do not take credit for someone else's work is an important part of training students for the real world. Teaching students to avoid plagiarism and how to cite sources is an important step in having them know when to take credit and when to give credit to others.

There are a few other strategies I've employed that have helped me to prevent students from feeling the need to plagiarize papers. I make sure that I do not assign any research project until I have had students submit to me many different examples of their writing.

A lesson plan for teaching students to cite sources can be found at http://www.readwritethink.org/lessons/lesson_view .asp?id=158. Consult the following websites for further information on the proper way to cite sources: http://citationmachine .net/, http://www.easybib.com, and http://www.noodletools .com.

During the course of the school year, I have students write a lot. It might be a descriptive essay or just an opportunity to report and comment on a book they have read. By requiring that students submit many different examples of their writing to me, I get an idea of each student's writing style and also teach lessons on various traits of effective writing. I have many examples of each student's writing before I assign the I-search paper. Knowing a student's strengths and weaknesses when it comes to writing assignments helps me to find evidence of plagiarism in his I-search paper. Students who are insecure in their writing abilities may be tempted to "borrow" the words and phrases of more able writers, recognizing that they may not be as skillful. But I assure students that I want to hear their voices, their ideas, their interpretations of the information they've found, and that simply copying the sentences of another writer simply won't do. I foster a writers' workshop atmosphere when they work on their drafts in class, so I can confer with individuals to see how they can make the information their own by using their own words. Just in case someone might plagiarize, it's seldom difficult for me to spot. If previous assignments have demonstrated that a student has problems with descriptive phrases or conventions, yet his I-search paper is free from punctuation mistakes and filled with meaty description and good word choice, it signals a red flag for me. Because so much of the I-search paper relies on voice, I can see if a student uses the same voice in his I-search paper that he has used in previous writing samples. Having various samples of the student's writing helps me determine whether the work is actually his or someone else's. Then I prefer to address the issue with the individual student so that this can be corrected, rather than simply wielding the sword of a failing grade.

Another thing that I do is to help keep students from feeling any time pressures that sometimes lead to plagiarism or stealing papers. I pick the due date for the project so that it does not coincide with large projects or tests in other classes. This requires communication with the other eighth-grade teachers, but fortunately, as we have weekly team meetings, this is not a problem. When students have several big projects or tests scheduled at the same time, plagiarism or cheating becomes a very attractive method to ensure that everything gets done on time. Scheduling also means that I need to be aware of athletic or cultural events that may be happening just prior to when a project is due. Most middle school students I know have a problem keeping a balance between schoolwork and activities. But we want kids to have time for fun as well as academic endeavors. If there is a big track meet or a band competition, I realize that most students may have a problem keeping their focus on academics. By making sure that they are not overwhelmed with schoolwork at the same time that another big activity is vying for their time assures me that a student will give my assignment the attention it needs.

Even the most conscientious teacher has had a case where plagiarism has been suspected. Many schools subscribe to turnitin.com or other services that allow teachers to compare student work to a database that will show evidence of plagiarism. Some of these results have been amazing. However, many teachers do not have the ability to use a Web-based product. Fortunately, while the Internet can aid students in finding material to plagiarize, it also can help teachers to find evidence when plagiarism is suspected. One way is for teachers to try typing phrases from suspected papers into search engines. Using the same strategy to check online databases is a way to determine if a student has plagiarized from a periodical or online reference source.

For information on using Google or other search engines to detect plagiarism, consult the following website: http://www .marywood.edu/library/detectplag.htm.

I know other teachers who have their own ideas for combating plagiarism. Some teachers require that all the actual writing be done in the classroom or under supervision in a writing lab or computer lab. Doing all the actual writing in school rather than outside the classroom can certainly cut down on wholesale plagiarism. It assures the teacher that the work is the student's own without help from a parent or another person. This method could work well with short assignments and also with projects that require instruction in word processing techniques, such as the career recruitment brochure that was mentioned in chapter 6.

Other teachers often require that students use a specific number of different sources; for instance, they may require that the students use at least three books, two online sources, and no more than four websites. Some may require that at least one source must have been published during the last year. In looking at my students' bibliographies, I make sure that most of the sources they have used for information are available in the school library. Bibliographies with lots of unfamiliar titles can signal that someone else who did not have access to our school library wrote the paper. Because many purchased or online research papers do not have these restrictions and because the sources from these stolen papers are sometimes dated, this is another strategy to circumvent plagiarism.

Some teachers require weekly evidence that the students are doing the research by using a weekly checklist or point system to make sure that their students are actually doing the work assigned. Some of the checklist examples provided in chapter 4 could be modified for this purpose. Not only do students accumulate points on the checklist for doing the work, the work is spread over a specific time period. Students are less likely to purchase or steal papers when they know that they need to demonstrate systematic progress in their research to their teacher. The checklist method also allows the teacher to determine those students who are having difficulty along the way, so it serves a double purpose. Having students turn in parts of the project over a set time period not only keeps students on task and helps to discourage plagiarism, it also encourages students to complete work on time and learn important time management skills that will be important as they go on to college.

I know teachers who require their students to submit photocopies of all the information they have used from books or magazines and printouts of any information they have found on the Web when they turn in their final paper. Although this may give these teachers an idea of where students got their information, I feel that students could conveniently forget to print out the information on the website they used to plagiarize their information. Many require that students highlight the sections of information that they used in their papers. Then the teachers look for the evidences of this in the students' papers. With either of these strategies I would find the pages of paper unmanageable. Although making all these copies might be a windfall of revenue for the school library, I think it is an unnecessary waste of trees.

Another method some teachers use to combat plagiarism is to require that students provide an annotated bibliography of the resources they have used in researching their topic. In order to produce an annotated bibliography, students must actually look at a resource. Requiring an annotated bibliography also helps to prevent the "padding" of bibliographies with resources that cover the topic but that the student did not actually use.

I require that my students do a "creative piece" to accompany the I-search paper. These creative pieces often take the form of oral reports or posters that students cannot possibly plagiarize. Adding an oral component to the research project is another way to combat plagiarism. When teachers create a different way to demonstrate the results of student research,

such as writing a skit or creating a newspaper, or when teachers use assignments that do not take the form of an expository report or term paper, plagiarism can be minimized. The next chapter provides teachers with a variety of projects that can be assigned other than the traditional research paper.

I have had few students resort to plagiarism for my I-search assignment. They are far more likely to plagiarize on shorter assignments or ones that do not interest them, like writing poetry. Although written papers are the easiest to plagiarize, I find the I-search format can make it more difficult for students to find entire papers online. In addition, this multiweek project gives my students time to really learn information literacy skills that can be transferred to shorter assignments or creative projects in the future. It also allows me to monitor my students and help them out every step of the way.

FURTHER READING

For more information on methods to combat plagiarism and to design assignments that are difficult to plagiarize, consult the following books and articles:

DeSena, Laura Hennessey. *Preventing Plagiarism: Tips and Techniques.* Urbana, IL: National Council of Teachers of English, 2007.

Don't let students "overlook" Internet plagiarism. *Education Digest* (October 2004): 37–43.

Harris, Robert A. *The Plagiarism Handbook.* Los Angeles, CA: Pyrczak, 2001.

Lathrop, Ann, and Kathleen Foss. *Student Cheating and Plagiarism in the Internet Era: A Wakeup Call.* Englewood, CO: Libraries Unlimited, 2000.

Loertscher, David V., Carol Koechlin, and Sandi Zwaan. *Ban Those Bird Units!* Salt Lake City, UT: Hi-Willow Research, 2005.

McKenzie, Jamie. *Beyond Technology: Questioning, Research, and the Information Literate School.* Seattle, WA: FNO Press, 2000.

Miller-Widrick, Melinda. Preventing plagiarism. *Cable in the Classroom* (May 2007): 8–9.

For a PowerPoint presentation on plagiarism that can be shared with students, consult the following:

Valenza, Joyce Kazman. *Power Tools Recharged: 125+ Essential Forms and Presentations for Your School Library Information Program.* Chicago: American Library Association, 2004.

For information on how to motivate students without emphasizing grades, consult:

Kohn, Alfie. *Punished by Rewards: The Trouble with Gold Stars Incentive Plans, A's, Praise, and Other Bribes.* New York: Houghton Mifflin, 1999.

Teachers who are interested in additional tips on preventing plagiarism, should consult the following website: http://www.virtualsalt.com/antiplag.htm.

11

Not Another Boring Report!

This book has focused on a long-range research project that can take four to six weeks of a forty-minute class. I know that this I-search project prepares students for future research-related experiences that may be assigned when they go on to high school or college. I know that taking the time to monitor students' research now and making sure that my I-search assignment gives them a positive research experience will pay dividends because my students will be prepared whenever they are faced with an information need in the future. So I don't skimp, and I monitor my students every step of the way.

Some teachers may be throwing up their hands and thinking, "This sounds great . . . but I can't devote that much time to a project like this one." Certainly there are other projects that can require students to learn important research skills but need teachers to devote just a few days for the project. Tailoring a research project that will meet the needs of your students and fit into the constraints of your calendar can be a worthwhile endeavor. Several suggestions for alternate research projects have been mentioned in earlier chapters—the endangered species project or chemical elements brochure mentioned in chapter 1, for example. Many of these ideas for alternate projects require students to use information literacy skills. They expose students to many different resources that are available to them for finding information. Yet many of these alternative projects can be accomplished in a week or two of class time. In fact, the careers project mentioned in chapter 6 is a one-week project for me.

Other teachers may say, "But what about creating projects that use technology?" Certainly, research does not mean that the final product needs to be the written report. Students love the "bells and whistles" of technology, so they enjoy using technology to show what they've learned. Research projects certainly can use tech-

nology. No matter what shape or form your final product takes, some things are universal. You want to create a project that will be filled with ideas, that demonstrates that a student researcher has a strong understanding of the topic, and that shows that the student has thought critically, has evaluated information and resources, and has drawn conclusions. Following solid procedures during the research process will result in meaty presentations or projects whether the form is a written paper or a project that employs technology.

Sometimes I require my students to also prepare a creative project to extend what they learned while doing the I-search paper. Figure 11.1 is an example of the handout I prepared that extends this I-search project. This handout gives students an idea of several creative ways that they can share what they learned about their topic through their research. It allows my students to be creative and gives them ideas for how to fashion the information they gained as a result of the project into something other than a written report. These ideas also provide for ways that the results of their information search can be shared with the rest of the class.

As long as students have the requisite information literacy skills that allow them to extract information from many sources and can turn this information into new knowledge that can be communicated to others, there are many types of assignments that can be given. During my years of teaching, some of my colleagues have developed assignments that offer other creative ways of having students demonstrate the knowledge they acquired while researching a topic. Some of these creative projects have been quite successful and have subsequently been used each year as part of the curriculum by the teachers who developed them. The projects can take anywhere from a few days to a few weeks to produce the desired result. Successful creative projects can be written, oral, artistic, or computer based.

CONCERNS PROJECT – THE CREATIVE PART

You have now become an expert on your topic and have written a paper that shows all that you know. Now it is time to share your information in a creative way with your classmates. You will prepare a creative piece that you will show and explain to the class in order to educate them on the topic and perhaps to convince them to share your opinion or even to take some action regarding your topic.

Some ideas for your project include:
- Write and perform a skit. (You may include others in your skit, but you must write the skit on your own and practice it outside of school time. We will not have time during the school day to practice skits in class.)
(You may put your skit on videotape and show it to the class or perform the skit live!)
- Create an imaginary person who has been affected by the issue you have researched. Prepare and deliver a monologue in this person's voice.
- Write letters or a diary that this person might have written and read it to the class.
- Write and perform a news broadcast, a TV interview, or a talk show (NOT Jerry Springer style!) that addresses your issue. (Remember, there will be NO practice time available during the school day.)
- Write a collection of poetry about your issue.
- Write a short story.
- Write a dialog between two people.
- Write a description of a situation from two or more points of view.
- Create a CD that focuses on your issue. Include song titles and some lyrics of a few songs that focus on the issue.
- Write letters expressing your views and mail them to lawmakers or the local newspaper. Find the appropriate addresses and express your concern to people who can make a difference. Use a correct business letter format and style. (See <u>Write Source</u> book.) Then read your letters to the class.
- Make an educational poster.
- Create a fictional front page of a newspaper that features articles or stories about the issue.
- Create an informational brochure.
- Create editorial cartoons that express your opinion on the topic. Explain them to the class.
- Be imaginative! Create some other way of educating your classmates.

ASSESSMENT OF PROJECT
You will present your project to the class. You will be assessed on the combination of the project you prepare and the presentation that you make in class. The class should learn new and thorough information from the combination of project and presentation.

Fig. 11.1. A handout that extends this I-search project.

RESEARCH PROJECTS
WITH A WRITTEN COMPONENT

When writing a full-length research paper may be too daunting or time consuming, creating an annotated bibliography is an excellent way to help students learn about the many different resources in the school library that students will encounter in their research. It can also teach them how to evaluate these resources. For example, students could begin by selecting a topic of interest and then find three periodical articles dealing with the topic chosen. Annotated bibliographies can take several different forms, but all require that the student creating the annotated bibliography record each source using proper bibliographic form and include a short paragraph that summarizes the information found. Teachers can allow students to include any type of information resource in the annotated bibliography or they can tailor the types of resources chosen to give students exposure to those with which they are unfamiliar. The number of sources required for the bibliography can be set to a specific number to fit time constraints. Requiring that students also include a few paragraphs that compare and contrast the resources rather than just summarizing the information found in each extends the project and mandates that students employ critical thinking skills.

Creating newspapers—or even just the front page—can be the end product of research. A history teacher can ask students to create a newspaper on a particular era, such as the Great Depression. Or students could create a newspaper that might be written by citizens in one of the original thirteen colonies. I have seen some student-created newspapers on a particular decade, such as the 1950s. Such newspapers feature important news events, cultural trends, and fashion. After looking at copies of the magazine *Kids Discover*, students could create a similar type of magazine that includes text and pictures on a particular topic. Magazines done for science class could include topics such as weather or an endangered animal; for health class, a magazine on nutrition, fitness, or first aid could be done.

Having students write letters is another way to demonstrate understanding of a topic. Students can assume the persona of an immigrant and write letters to a friend or family member describing the new things they have experienced in another country or the ways the new country is different from their native land. Postcards that describe similar impressions or that offer facts about a foreign country can extend the geography or foreign language classes. Students can also use letters to express opinions or motivate others to action. Letters to editors or lawmakers to ask their support on an issue or a persuasive letter encouraging others to take action on a community or national issue is a logical follow-up to research.

After researching an issue, students have the background information needed to create compelling fiction stories that illustrate the dilemmas faced by individuals who are involved in an issue that has been researched. Creating a fictional character pushes the writer to put a human face on a problem that may have only been facts or figures before. For example, a student could take on the persona of an eighth grader with juvenile diabetes and describe the challenges that a teen with this disease might face in school during the course of a week. Students can learn to embed these stories with the thoughts and feeling of the characters, to use dialog that moves the story along, and to include plenty of description of both actions and events. These written pieces are enriched with themes and realistic conflicts that can educate others on the problems faced by other people. An example of a fiction story written by an eighth grader that dramatizes an important issue is provided in appendix B.

Many students enjoy reading books written in journal or diary format. Another suggestion is to have students create fictional journals that demonstrate a theme. For example, after studying organ donation, a student could take on the persona of a teen needing a organ transplant and journal his thoughts and feelings, describing what led up to his illness, describing his ordeal, and providing readers with important facts about organ donation.

RESEARCH PROJECTS
WITH AN ORAL COMPONENT

Do your students enjoy performing? Creating a skit, interview, or a talk show allows students to present information and practice their acting skills as well. As long as the topics aren't stolen from Jerry Springer, this can be an entertaining way for students to demonstrate their knowledge on a topic. Allowing students to produce a documentary on videotape may be just the thing to motivate reluctant writers who enjoy performing but hate writing papers.

Advertising is a pervasive fact of life in our world. Why not tie in a study of advertisers' persuasive techniques with the creation of a public service advertisement that will lead an audience to a particular point of view? An excellent way to tie in a media literacy unit with research is to have students create a public service advertisement/announcement that educates the public on an important issue, such as the dangers of smoking or the need to recycle trash. Students enjoy having an opportunity to make themselves heard on issues that are important to them. A public service announcement can be much more than a print ad. Students can create video productions that teach others about the issue they've studied. Writing a script, developing a storyboard, creating a slogan, and then producing the advertisement involves the integration of reading, writing, and technology skills that make this assessment a rich one.

I have successfully had my eighth-grade students design and write public service advertisements in my classroom. Figure 11.2 introduces this assignment to my class. This handout also serves as an assignment organizer that gets them focused on what they need to do to complete the project. I make sure that students fill out this form and hand it in before they begin the actual work of researching the issue and composing the public service advertisement.

The class enjoys viewing public service announcements, whether in video or presented "in person." Because they are short in length, these presentations only take a few days of class time. This assignment also gives the students a greater appreciation for the advertisements that they see each day on television or hear on radio. They learn to focus on the important elements related to the topic, so that they can create a public service advertisement/announcement that fits into the time constraints of the project. This assignment also gives me an opportunity to teach about persuasion and bias. Students learn to look for these elements in the advertisements and commercials and have become more informed consumers. An example of a public service advertisement created by an eighth grader is provided in appendix C.

RESEARCH PROJECTS
WITH AN ARTISTIC COMPONENT

Another idea for a creative project as an alternative to a written report is to have students make a poster or bio-board. I know students who have created posters for social studies classes that depict their nomination of the "Person of the Decade." Similar to the *Time* magazine "Man of the Year," this poster presents photos and information on the person, as well as the reasons why the student feels he or she deserves this honor. Science classes could employ the same idea. Encouraging students to research and create a poster about a scientist whose achievements have made an important contribution to science and the world is an example of a research project for science class. Making sure that the students extend their knowledge beyond simply regurgitating facts is important in this type of assignment. Requiring that students include on the poster or in an additional written piece their assessment of the person's importance to the world of knowledge or by requiring

students to compare the person to another scientist or someone in another field is a way to ensure that students are not simply copying down facts but taking the information and reacting to it.

RESEARCH PROJECTS THAT
EMPLOY COMPUTER TECHNOLOGY

Kids love the opportunity to show off their technology skills. PowerPoint presentations are another example of how students can combine technology with research. A good PowerPoint presentation will demand that a student be able to determine what is most important about a topic so as not to overwhelm the audience with too much information. In order to create a presentation that will inform and entertain the audience, the student will need to know how to organize the information and make the slides interesting.

Creating brochures is another way for students to record information they have found while using computer skills. The career brochure in chapter 6 is one example that I have used that demonstrates this type of assignment. I have students choose a career. They then create questions they want to answer about the career, including what type of education is required, what is involved in the job, and what types of responsibilities the career entails. After gathering information from career books and career software, the students design a brochure that explains why the career would be an appealing choice for others to consider. The writing trait of voice becomes especially important in this assignment. The writer of the brochure needs to convince the person looking over the brochure that the career is worth his consideration. Because the brochure is created in the computer lab, it is an excellent way for students to learn and practice computer design skills as well. This project gives me a chance to collaborate with the school's technology teacher, who is best equipped to give me an idea of what computer skills the students will need to learn in order to produce an appealing brochure. This assignment allows students to expand their technology skills as well as their information literacy and writing skills.

Because a brochure can be informational or persuasive in tone, opportunities to present information in brochure format can be found in other areas of the curriculum as well. Students can create travel brochures to demonstrate their knowledge of the economics, government, or important landmarks of a country for geography class. A brochure that could be published by a government agency, such as information on the Constitution or things an immigrant should know before becoming a citizen, are ideas that could be used in a social studies class. Depending on the era the students are

Name _____ Date _____

CREATING A PUBLIC SERVICE ADVERTISEMENT

Choose an issue that you feel strongly about. Create a public service advertisement that expresses your point of view on this issue and that persuades your audience.

Prepare a 2 to 3 minute talk that gives your audience some background information on the topic.

Next you will show them your public service advertisement and explain it to them.

You will be assessed on the following criteria:

Talk: Ideas – filled with important and accurate information

PSA: Voice; Conventions, including professional appearance

List the main pieces of information you will explain in the talk that you will give:

_____

_____

_____

_____

_____

_____

_____

What is the issue your PSA will address?

_____

Who is your target audience? (Although you will be speaking to your classmates, you may act as if they are a different type of audience; for example, parents of teens.)

_____

What is the main point that you want your PSA to express?

_____

_____

_____

_____

(over .....)

_____

Why do you believe that this is an important idea or message?

_____

Fig. 11.2.   A handout that introduces this assignment to my class.

_____

_____

_____

_____

_____

What persuasive techniques will you use to persuade your audience?

_____

_____

_____

_____

_____

_____

★★★★★★★★★★★★

In the space below, do a sketch of your advertisement.

Fig. 11.2. *Continued*

studying in American history class, a brochure meant to entice settlers to head west or to encourage citizens to support the war effort are other examples of assignments that could be used by history teachers. Science teachers could ask students to create a brochure on a chemical element or one that outlines safety procedures to follow in a lab.

Creating a website is another effective way to blend research skills with technology use. A student-created website can give an overview of a topic and also provide users with links to follow to other websites for additional information. Not only does this website assignment require that students use search engines and other resources to find websites on their topic, it also forces them to evaluate information contained in websites, an important information literacy skill that is especially important for students to master in the Internet age. An assignment like this also may provide students with instruction in HTML or other skills that will aid them in the online environment. These student-produced websites can be easily shared with other students.

When creating a website may be too time consuming, having students create a blog can be a way for students to post the results of their information search on the Internet. Creating a class wiki and having students contribute to it is another online tool that can be used for publishing the results of student research.

These are just a few suggestions of creative projects that require students to employ information literacy skills but are different from the traditional written research paper. Another advantage of using a creative project to report the results of research is that these types of projects are much harder to copy or plagiarize. Creative teachers can find numerous examples of creative projects on the Internet, on library or teacher listservs, or by consulting the teacher-librarian or technology teacher for suggestions.

The amount and type of research needed for these examples of creative assignments vary in depth and breadth, but each can be the impetus to teaching how to develop a topic, how to create questions, find sources, take notes, give credit to sources, and how to organize information into a meaningful form. The important thing to keep in mind when designing any type of project is the essential question, "What will students learn and be able to do when this project is completed?" By

Many teachers use http://www.wikispaces.com/ as a means for students to contribute to a wiki or blog.

An extensive list of alternatives to a written research paper can be accessed at http://mciunix.mciu.k12.pa.us/~spjvweb/fiftyways.html.

focusing on this question, teachers will be better prepared to anticipate what strategies and skills will need to be taught and practiced along the way.

FURTHER READING

For more ideas on alternative assignments, consult these sources:

Loertscher, David V., Carol Koechlin, and Sandi Zwaan. *Ban Those Bird Units!* Salt Lake City, UT: Hi-Willow Research, 2005.

Stanley, Deborah B. *Practical Steps to the Research Process for Elementary School.* Englewood, CO: Libraries Unlimited, 2001.

Stanley, Deborah B. *Practical Steps to the Research Process for High School.* Englewood, CO: Libraries Unlimited, 1999.

Valenza, Joyce Kazman. *Power Tools Recharged: 125+ Essential Forms and Presentations for Your School Library Information Program.* Chicago: American Library Association, 2004.

12

When Will I Ever Use This Stuff?

It seems that each year school administrators are becoming more concerned with the results of mandated standardized tests than the critical thinking skills and reading strategies that our students should be learning. Although the percentage points of students meeting state test requirements might be inching upward, there are lots of curricular casualties along the way. One of these is having adequate time to teach students important information literacy skills and giving them assignments that require them to search for information in various types of primary and secondary sources. With a focus on making sure students get the requisite knowledge to score well on standardized tests, it seems that providing students with the opportunity to explore a subject of interest, to find usable and interesting information to make one's own, has been squeezed out of the school day. Yet this has never been more important.

Teaching research does not deserve to go by the wayside. To develop students who will have the skills to be successful in the twenty-first century, it is essential that information literacy skills not be forfeited in favor of higher test scores. Michael B. Eisenberg, one of the developers of Big6, has stated that library media information skills may actually help students do better on standardized tests (Eisenberg 2004). Students need the ability to comprehend questions and choose between several responses. Reading strategies that are taught can be employed on standardized tests. Content knowledge is important but so are reasoning and critical thinking skills. Well-developed research projects can help students learn how to sift through information, decide on the best answer, and relate knowledge to what has been taught.

Data, data, everywhere! Every news broadcast, every newspaper, every commercial, every magazine ad, every website seems filled with statistics. Want to know the passing efficiency of your favorite NFL quarterback? You need only go to http://www.nfl.com. Broadcast newscasts are filled with numbers. How many U.S. military personnel have been killed in Iraq, how much the price of gas has increased in the past year—these are all statistics that are reported to a listening public. Along with statistics, "facts" abound. There is "factual" information everywhere about the crisis in the Middle East, about the candidates who are running for state governor, about the most healthful yogurt, about the love life of Tom and Katie. How do we weed through all of this? What information is reliable and what is purely marketing or gossip? Because we are on data overload, reading through information and determining what is accurate and important is a life skill students need to survive in the twenty-first century.

The Partnership for 21st Century Skills recently released a study that looked at the skills that high school students would need to succeed in college and in life. Among the findings in this study is the realization that high schools are not imparting the kinds of higher level thinking skills that are becoming increasingly important in a competitive world economic environment. One of the six key elements that the partnership has identified for twenty-first-century learning is "the need to know how to keep learning—and make effective and innovative use of what they know—throughout their lives." Taking these findings into consideration builds credence for the importance of well-crafted research opportunities because a critical part of this learning is that students need to develop information and literacy skills before entering college.

The full results of this study can be accessed at http://www.21stcenturyskills.org.

The need for students to master information literacy skills was further supported by a study by Achieve, Inc. in association with Peter D. Hart Research Associates that was reported in the October 2005 issue of *Teacher/*

Librarian. Researchers found that most recent high school graduates indicated that they lacked important research skills. Certainly these studies reveal that giving students in middle and high school the opportunity to learn information literacy skills and structuring assignments that require that students demonstrate the use of these important skills will set them up for success in post–high school endeavors and in life.

> Results of the entire project can be accessed at http://www .achieve.org.

What happens when students do not encounter their very first research assignment until they are in college? For novices to the process, a research task can look impossibly daunting. Just imagine the thoughts going through the mind of someone who has never been taught how to search for and synthesize information. "Where do I start? What do I need to look for? How will I keep track of all the stuff I find? Why do two different sources say two different things? Who is right? How do I share what I find with others in an understandable way?" Students who have been exposed to only teacher-delivered, lock-step instruction may throw up their hands in despair before they even begin. On the other hand, some students who are unfamiliar with information literacy skills may just think research is easy. "What's the big deal?" they may say. "I'll just Google my topic and cut and paste." So, with tons of confidence and lots of naiveté, they log on to the magic land of the Internet, assuming that everything they find will be accurate and valuable. Copying a paragraph here, pasting another paragraph there, ignoring sources, this student will patch together "research" without any true understanding of the topic or the process.

Researching is not only important for college survival. Will our students need to elect a governor, senator, or president in the future? Then they will need to wade through campaign declarations in order to make an intelligent choice based on the issues. Will our students ever purchase a home, buy a car, plan a vacation, and make a decision about medical needs or investments? Will they wish to make sense of new technology, world issues, or new challenges that the future brings their way? Will they get jobs that demand that they learn about other cultures? The information literacy skills that they develop through well-planned research projects will help them with all these challenges. Finding pertinent information and using critical thinking skills are not only an academic endeavor.

We cannot leave the teaching of research to chance. Students benefit from multiple opportunities of doing their own research—getting their hands dirty, so to speak. Finding information, separating fact from fiction, recognizing bias, and determining what is important are essential life skills. Students need the time and the opportunity to walk down the paths of research on their own, stumbling along the way, taking detours, rethinking their direction, grappling with opposing viewpoints to get the true flavor of what it means to research. They need to understand that research can be "messy." Yet with each challenge, real learning takes place—learning that can be transferred the next time an information need crops up.

Just as there is no one "right way" to conduct research, it is imperative for classroom teachers and teacher-librarians to realize that a curriculum that enriches students' information literacy skills should scaffold on previous skills learned, building on students' previous research experiences, adding more and more sophisticated tools to their research toolboxes. Simply doing that old chestnut, "the sophomore term paper," is not enough to develop a mastery of research skills. We learn by doing—not just once, but many times. A sixth grader, for example, may put together a class newspaper on Ancient Greece. A seventh grader might lay out a trip down the Danube River, pointing out the important cities and places of interest along the way. By eighth grade, the I-search paper on a current topic of concern will further test students' research skills. By the time sophomore year rolls around, a student will have a varied and increasingly complex set of research experiences to draw upon. By college, the student who is confident with his information literacy skills will focus on learning more about a topic from the information that is found rather than just learning how to research it.

I have chosen to make an I-search project part of my eighth-grade language arts curriculum. Although a written paper may seem "archaic" as a means to teach students information literacy skills, I am, after all, a "writing" teacher. The I-search paper allows me to not only systematically teach my students the steps to research, it also give me an opportunity to assess the writing skills they possess. Additionally, this project gives my students the opportunity to learn the differences between print material and that found on the Internet. It teaches them the importance of a questioning mind and the value of being organized and systematic. Certainly, this project is not as "flashy" as having students contribute to a class wiki, but it does work for me. The methods I employ and handouts I use—from the assignment organizer to the thinking logs—are things that can be used by any teacher who is assigning a research project, no matter if the project is a written assignment, an oral report, or some other way of demonstrating research findings. The important thing is that students be given the proper instruction in information literacy skills, time needed to adequately learn and use them, and opportunities to produce a quality assignment that demonstrates their research abilities. I know that giving my students this opportunity to research will pay big dividends when they are taking tests, making decisions, and relating to others. The information literacy skills they are developing in my classroom as part of my research assignments are essential to their becoming well-rounded, literate adults. And that is the important thing—not what form the assignment may take.

FURTHER READING

For more information about the importance of information literacy skills and lifelong learning, consult the following sources:

Appel, Justin. Report: Students struggle with information literacy. *eSchoolNews online* (November 2006), at http://eschoolnews.com (accessed August 30, 2007).

Eisenberg, Michael B. It's all about learning: Ensuring that students are. *Library Media Connection* (March 2004): 22–30.

Fitzgerald, Mary Ann. Making the leap from high school to college. *Knowledge Quest* (March–April 2004): 19–24.

High school and college: The skills disconnect. *Teacher Librarian* (October 2005): 33.

Taylor, Joie. *Information Literacy and the School Library Media Center.* Westport, CT: Libraries Unlimited, 2006.

Weis, June Pullen. Contemporary literacy skills. *Knowledge Quest* (March–April 2004): 12–15.

Appendix A

Sample Eighth-Grade I-Search Report

DYING TO BE PERFECT

On a quest for perfection, many women, and even men, develop one of the few psychological diseases with most of the results harming them physically. Anorexia nervosa takes the lives of 10–20% of its victims. But there are ways that they can be helped before damaging their bodies permanently both physically and mentally.

Anorexia nervosa is basically defined as extreme starvation that leads to a catastrophic weight loss but, as you read on, you will find that there are many more characteristics that describe and define anorexia. The word anorexia means "lack of appetite," when, in actuality, an anorexic is starving. "Nervosa" means having to do with the nerves.

There are actually two types of anorexia. The restricting type uses methods of dieting, fasting, and excessive exercise to lose weight. The second type is known as the binge-eating/purging type. It is very complicated because it is often confused with bulimia but an anorexic with this type of anorexia will binge-eat and then purge by vomiting. They will often misuse laxatives, diuretics, or enemas. The anorexic may even purge regularly after eating small amounts of food.

There is too vast a number of people with sub-clinical, or threshold, eating disorders. They are people who are much too preoccupied with food and weight but their abnormal behaviors aren't disturbed enough to qualify for a formal diagnosis. Despite those large amounts of people, about 1% of women between the ages of 15 and 30 are suffering from anorexia. In other words, one out of every 100 women between the ages 15 and 30 has been formally diagnosed with anorexia.

Anorexia typically begins to develop between the ages of 12 to 14 or later at age 17 into the 20s. Despite the typical age, it does not mean that anyone who is younger or older cannot develop anorexia. In fact, there have been cases reported in people as old as 76 years

old or as young as 6 years old. Anorexia also seems to run in families: A girl who has a sibling with the disease has a 10 to 20 times greater risk of developing it than the average girl her age.

Anorexia is usually associated with women because for women, thin is popular and society shows us that to be attractive, women need to be thin. On the other hand, society tells us that a man who is large and muscular is popular. That makes many people think that men don't suffer from anorexia. Actually, about 5–10% of the total number of people with anorexia are males. The risk factors for males are similar to females, being that they were fat or overweight as children, they have been dieting, they participate in a sport that demands thinness (such as horse-racing or gymnastics), or they have a job or profession that demands thinness (such as modeling). Males often begin an eating disorder at older ages than females. Men are often reluctant to admit that they are in trouble and need help because eating disorders are described as female problems. Men also say that they feel out of place in discussions centered on such female issues as the loss of menstrual periods.

Those who have been studying the spread of anorexia have found that age and gender are closely related to the development of the disease but ethnic background and economic status are not. Despite this, there is still a defined stereotypical anorexic that seems to prevail. These people are usually well dressed, go to the best schools, and have been introduced to cultural activities at a very young age. Although they are not necessarily brilliant or gifted, anorexics are generally superior students. They and their parents are proud of their academic achievements.

Many anorexics seem to be from "perfect" homes. They are mainly upper-middle-class environments where a large amount of attention is directed in satisfying material needs as well as other family members.

Their families are close-knit and don't allow each other much room for individuality. In fact, as a young child, the anorexic is strongly discouraged from becoming his or her own person with a broad range of feelings and emotions that are common to all humans. Instead they must become a model of perfection that reflects only the qualities that their parents deem desirable. They are expected to shine athletically and academically and to perform brilliantly in all areas of their life.

Because their parents give them so much, anorexics feel that they must live up to unrealistically high expectations to please their family, teachers, and friends. They feel they must do well in life to repay their family for the advantages that they have been given. The anorexic will display perfect manners and behavior and is very polite at all times as an unconscious payback to their parents. The anorexic will frequently resort to inordinate ways not to offend or disappoint his or her parents in even the smallest way. They are frightened about not doing well enough and are almost haunted by the irrational fear of failure.

Anorexics put far more effort into winning and maintaining friendships than the average young person does. They are overly compliant in their relationships with almost anyone. They are people-pleasers at almost any cost to themselves. They will continually go out of their way to please and do extras for someone, almost to the point of servitude. Although anorexics want to please everyone, they often have one very close friend to which they may devote lots of effort to become like. Anorexics want to be accepted and are very concerned with what people think of them. The impression that they make on others is foremost in their mind. They will constantly compare themselves to others, but will never feel superior.

The families of anorexics tend to be small, often with only 1 or 2 children. It seems that most anorexics don't have brothers, and if they do, they are often a number of years younger. The parents are often older than the average parent when the child who becomes an anorexic was born. In many cases, the mother was in her late 30s or early 40s when the child was born. The parents also give as much as they possibly can to provide a fulfilling and harmonious home life. They both speak with tremendous pride when describing the "ideal" child that they helped to mold. Mothers are generally conscientious parents who are genuinely concerned with rearing their children correctly. Many mothers were professionals who gave up their careers for a while to devote herself more to the children. The mother will become overly involved in her child's life and in return for her costly and personal investment, the child feels he or she must please her. Studies on the mothers have shown that they appear to be secure and self-assured on the surface. They are often very concerned with the appearance of their home and family. They place a lot of emphasis on making themselves appear as physically attractive as possible, almost to the point of obsession. In families with no sons, the fathers tend to put unrealistic expectations on their daughters. At a young age, the fathers will hold their daughters responsible for "carrying on the family name." He does not expect this through marriage, of course, but through achievements.

People who develop anorexia seem to have an underlying "core" problem that started their anorexia. As an example, teenagers who have enormous amounts of pressure put on them and who are not encouraged to become their own person will often rebel by not eating. Or, as another example, a teenager who is being severely abused can only seem to deal with his or her problem by not eating. But there is often something that actually triggers them to stop eating. Anorexia will often start with some sort of comment pertaining to a person's weight, such as, "You really could lose a few pounds." The person will begin to diet, enjoying the positive feedback and sense of control she has over her body. Somehow, they begin to lose perspective on what a healthy and attractive body really is and they continue to diet. What started out as a simple diet to lose a few pounds develops into anorexia. Many teen female anorexics are often described as fearful of growing up. By fasting, they find that they can keep their breasts and hips from developing normally and block the process of menstruation. One of the most powerful triggers of anorexia for men and women is simply dieting.

The greatest achievement for an anorexic is thinness. To do this, they basically starve themselves, the hunger making them feel thin. Many anorexics claim that they actually enjoy the sensations of hunger, stating that the pangs let them know that they aren't gaining any weight. Anorexics feel in control of their body and therefore somewhat in control of their life. As Stella expresses it, "When I was able to lose weight and keep it off, I finally felt as though I was in charge of my own welfare. It was strange, but wonderful—a sort of powerful feeling."

An anorexic cannot take chances. They can't eat one serving of something without feeling like they are going to blow up. They are comfortable only when their stomach is empty. Anorexics are not disgusted by food. As a matter of fact, food dominates their thoughts and they will do everything with it except eat it. They'll cook it, shop for it, read about it, and constantly think about it. But an anorexic does not realize the value of food for his or her body. The effect of intake of food is so distorted that she feels she must rigidly control what she eats.

A number of psychological effects come with anorexia, such as obsessive-compulsive behavior, social isolation, revulsion toward fat and self-indulgence, compulsive and excessive exercising, and often a hidden depression. The most consistent feature of anorexia is denial. The victim is not sure how to deal with unsettling feelings. They think that admitting that there may be a problem or voicing the littlest bit of criticism of their home life would show betrayal of their parents. They are afraid to admit to anyone, even themselves, that they feel troubled in any way.

An anorexic's behavior not only affects her, but the rest of her family and friends. As one friend remembered about another friend who died of anorexia, "It is hard to decide just how much energy to expend on people who do not want to be recipients of my caring. Harder still to walk away and leave them to their own devices. Yet, I do know that someone who does not want help cannot be helped"—WF.

A husband's heartfelt e-mail shows just how hard it is for both him and his wife, who suffers from anorexia accompanied by a severe case of over-exercising. "I am the husband of a lovely woman who is addicted to the exercise bike. She is a very beautiful woman, smart and well educated. She rationalizes every bit of exercise she does, and it is never too much. It controls our lives, but she doesn't see it. She will not eat any fat in her diet and only tiny bits of protein.

"She spends about one and a half hours on the bike each and every day—more if I don't say something to her. If she cannot exercise, she cuts down on her food and eats even less than usual. She equates her self-worth with how she looks and the job she has.

"I have tried to be supportive. I tell her my love is not based on her weight or her paycheck but on who she is and what she brings to our relationship. Nothing I do seems to make a difference. I am tired of having to talk to my wife over the roar of the exercise bike. I don't want to hear another irrational excuse for her staying the way she is.

"I have seen pictures of her at a heavier weight, and to me she was beautiful. I have told her this, but my words fall on deaf ears that listen only to what the warped little voice in her head tells her about what she needs to be appreciated and of value to herself and others.

"I am in this till death do-us-part because that is what I promised I would do. She got your [ANRED's] address from a women's magazine, but that is as far as she has gotten to doing anything about her problem. I have printed out some of your [ANRED's] Web pages in hopes she will read them and take them to heart.

"My love for my wife grows stronger each day. I just can't be the strength for us both. I want to fight this, but it is a battle inside her, and I can only help to pick her up when she falls. I can tell her I am here for her, but the battle is hers to fight. I desperately hope she will turn and confront the monster that controls her and tell it she will obey it no more. I write this for my wife, I LOVE YOU MY DARLING!!!"

Anorexics, themselves, suffer from the same things as people who suffer from involuntary malnutrition. Anorexics can suffer from insomnia, lack of concentration, indecisiveness, preoccupation with food, mood swings, irritability, and fatigue and lethargy.

Many physical affects of anorexia are things that can be easily noticed on the outside. A deprivation of protein will cause hair and nails to become brittle and dry. Hair may even begin to fall out. Vitamin deficiencies will eventually cause an anorexic's skin to become dry and scaly with a yellow or gray tint to it. Fine body hair, called lanugo, will grow as the anorexia progresses. The downy covering is probably an attempt by the body to keep warm by compensating for the loss of muscle and fat tissue. An anorexic also may develop constipation due to a water imbalance. Most anorexics cannot tolerate cool temperatures and always feel cold, especially their hands and feet.

The physical affects of anorexia can be long lasting and severe. As I stated before, it is one of the few psychological diseases with severe physical affects. The body's protective response to starvation is that the vital organ function declines, as if shifting into a lower gear of operation. Breathing and heart rates decline. Blood pressure will drop. Thyroid function slows. The body temperature goes down. Starvation also causes a breakdown in hormone production that can often result in osteoporosis, which is the loss of bone mass that leads to brittle bones. Osteoporosis in anorexics is comparable to the condition that develops in premenopausal women whose bodies have almost completely stopped producing estrogen. Long-term studies have found that osteoporosis that develops in older women cannot be reversed.

There are many crucial steps to the treatment of anorexia. For most patients, treatment is a long-term process. There are two important points that must be remembered before starting treatment. The first one is denial. Most anorexics refuse treatment so it is up to a family member or a friend to recognize the problem and get the patient into treatment before he or she is seriously damaged or dies. The second one is that continued monitoring and treatment is crucial because anorexia can be a chronic and reoccurring condition.

Most patients will go through psychological as well as medical treatments. Treatment may begin with hospitalization to deal with the physical effects of starvation on the body. Hospitalization is normally advised when patients are 70% of their recommended body weight, have rapidly progressing weight loss, have an irregular heart beat, have dizziness or fainting, and/or have low potassium levels.

The first step in treatment is "refeeding." Refeeding can be done on an in- or out-patient basis, depending on the severity of the condition and the cooperation of the patient. Some patients must be force-fed through nasogastric or intravenous tubes. The doctor will keep a close watch on symptoms such as abdominal bloating, constipation, and swelling, which can all develop during refeeding. These symptoms can be avoided or lessened if a more gradual approach is taken.

While refeeding goes on, the patient will begin behavioral therapy, psychotherapy, and nutritional counseling. Therapy is a lengthy process. A variety of approaches are used alone or in combination. It can include cognitive behavioral therapy and individual/group psychotherapy. Self-help groups are a major source of therapy for the patients. Family therapy has also become increasingly common because of the role that the family plays in the development of the disorder. Nutritional counseling is an absolutely crucial part of treatment.

A number of medications have been used to treat anorexia but no single one stands out. Antidepressants may be frequently prescribed if the patient has symptoms of depression. Anti-anxiety drugs have also worked in some cases.

People think if an anorexic gains weight she is cured. "But even though I looked healthier, I still struggled with cruel voices in my head that chanted *'You are a failure'*," Makenzie Stroh observed about her own recovery.

Anorexia is not necessarily cured by one successful treatment. "Cured" patients may suffer setbacks. Studies have found that 50% of anorexics who have been hospitalized for treatment and have gone through what may be considered a successful treatment will relapse.

Anorexia nervosa is fatal in up to 10% of the people who have it. The psychological and physical effects can be permanent. On the road to perfection, people are killing themselves with one of the most complex psychological diseases. Is it worth it to be perfect?

BIBLIOGRAPHY

ANRED. [Online] Available http://www.anred.com, 1998.

Landau, Elaine. *Why Are They Starving Themselves?* New York: Julian Messner, 1983.

Olson, Tod. "Images of Women: Should We All Be Like Kate?" *Scholastic Update*, March 8, 1996, 11.

The PDR Family Guide to Nutrition and Health. Montvale, New Jersey: Medical Economics Company, 1995.

Searles, John. "I Was Just 2 lbs. Away from Dying," *Cosmopolitan*, October 1997, 219–223.

Appendix B

Sample Eighth-Grade Fictional Story Based on Research

It was a cloudy, yet mild day for mid-January. Patches of melting snow covered the ground. The gray walls and barbed wire fences of the Tennessee State Prison stuck out against the black sky and the open farmland. The sniper and spotlight towers of the prison stood like mountains in the middle of nowhere. Deep inside, in cell 306, sat Thomas Sampson. Thomas was an African-American, about twenty-six years old, tall with square shoulder and a shaved head. Thomas had been married until his wife was murdered, and he was accused of the killing. Now as he sat in his cell, he kept thinking and thinking about the murder. Thomas knew what no one else knew. Not the prosecutors, not his neighbors, not even his own mother. Thomas knew the truth.

Thomas' thinking was interrupted as he heard the familiar clanking of the guard's keys. The guard stopped at Thomas' cell. Along with him was a tall, young man. He was freckled faced with brown hair and he wore a two-piece gray suit. He carried a black briefcase in his left hand and a wet umbrella in his right. The guard, leaving the man there, went back the way he came.

"Hello," said the man, extending his hand through the bars of the jail cell. Thomas grabbed his hand and shook it. The man noticed Thomas' firm grip. "My name is James Coron. I'll be representing you in court."

"Well, thank you. But I can't afford a lawyer."

"No problem. I'm court appointed. The county pays me. Let's get down to business." James pulled a chair standing in the corner up to the cell and opened his briefcase on his lap. Thomas sat on his cot and folded his hands.

"Let's see," started James. "You're accused of murder in the first degree for the stabbing death of your wife. Death penalty case. So we'll plead guilty to a lesser charge and get this thing over?"

"No," Thomas answered.

"What?" asked James, looking up from his papers.

"I'm innocent. I plead innocent."

"Well, that makes things interesting."

"I didn't kill Eve. I love her," said Thomas, almost whispering.

"They found evidence all over the place that points to you. How can you prove your innocence?"

"I saw the murder."

"We can't base this case on circumstantial evidence. We need proof."

"How long until the trial?" asked Thomas, leaning closer to James.

"Two days," he answered, loosening his tie. "Two days."

"Plenty of time, right?"

"I hope so. I really hope so."

The gavel banged loudly as the court was brought to order. The normal proceedings took place. The judge finally asked in a booming voice, "How does the defendant plead?"

James rose from his chair behind the bench and answered, "Innocent, Your Honor." A whisper moved through the jury as the white-haired judge banged the gavel loudly with a wrinkled hand.

"Thank you, Mr. Coron. Would the prosecution like to proceed?"

The district attorney, Sean Brown, stepped forward. He proceeded with police reports accounting the night of the murder. He presented a lab report showing that Thomas' fingerprints were found on the knife. He told the jury of Thomas' T-shirt, stained with the blood of Thomas' wife. The T-shirt was found in the trash. He ended the testimony stating there were no sounds of intrusion into Thomas' house.

"I would like to call Ms. Jennifer Walthrop to the stand," continued Sean. A middle-aged woman made her way to the stand. She had short, straight, brown hair, and wore a navy blue skirt and a matching blouse. She was quickly sworn in and took a seat.

"Ms. Walthrop," began Sean. "What were you doing on Friday, the 4th of January, 1999?"

"I left my house at 10 a.m. and ran some errands. I got back around 3 p.m. and spent the rest of the night at home."

"Did you notice anything unusual that night?"

"Yes. Yes, I did. I was watching TV around 10:30 p.m. The news or something. I heard this God-awful scream come from my neighbor's house."

"Which neighbors?"

"The Sampson's," she replied, obviously annoyed at the pointless question.

"Continue."

"I was frightened, so I called the police."

"Did you do anything until the police arrived?"

"I watched my neighbor's house. I don't know why, I just did."

"Did you notice anything unusual?"

She sat on the question for a while. "No . . . nothing."

"No further questions, Your Honor," finished Sean, returning to his seat.

"Thank you," said the judge. "Would you like to cross-examine the witness, Mr. Coron?"

"Yes, Your Honor," James replied, making his way to the stand. "Ms. Walthrop," he began, pacing the courtroom floor, "you said you didn't see anything unusual, correct?"

"Objection! We already covered this!" complained Sean.

"Overruled," muttered the judge.

"Yes, that's correct," breathed Jennifer, trying not to get caught in a lawyer's trap.

"Did you see anything at all? Any joggers passing, any cars sitting there?"

"No."

James was flustered by the response. He thought he could find something, anything. A getaway car, the murderer running away, anything. Instead, he hit a dead end. Just what he didn't want to do.

"No further questions," he said, head down, returning to the bench.

Now it was time for James to present their case. "Ladies and gentlemen. I feel my client to be truthful and innocent. First, the issue of the knife. My client had fallen asleep watching the TV the night of the murder. His wife shut off the television, leaving him in the basement, and she went to bed. My client awoke in the middle of the night to his wife's screams. He saw a car speed away from in front of his house. No license plates. Mr. Sampson ran up the stairs and found his wife with a knife in her back, bleeding to death. The criminal left no prints because he had gloves on. When my client pulled out the knife, he left his own prints.

"My client was obviously panicking at this time. He never thought of calling the police. The cause for his blood stained T-shirt can also be explained. My client tried, in a vain attempt, tried to stop his wife's bleeding, by using his T-shirt as a bandage and using it to apply pressure to the wound, obviously staining it with blood.

"Oh, yes. One final point. There was no sign of intrusion because my client did not lock his door that evening. His wife had a habit of never locking it, and he fell asleep on the couch. That is all."

The jurors whispered to each other and a few shook their heads. Both sides gave their closing arguments, summing up the facts and trying to persuade the jury one way or the other. The jury finally went in to decide Thomas' fate.

"James," said Thomas as James was standing to stretch. "The whole jury is white. There is not one black man on there."

James thought about that. It might help to push for a biased jury if there were any appeals.

"Don't worry, Thomas," replied James, sipping coffee from a Styrofoam cup. "Things will work out."

The jury returned after about twenty minutes of deliberating—a short time for a death penalty case. James prayed this wasn't a bad omen. The jurors took their seats while one of them brought the judge their decision. A man laid the paper down on the judge's desk with a heavy hand and returned to his seat.

The judge put on his large glasses prepared to hand out the decision.

"Would the defendant please rise?" asked the judge, motioning with a hand.

Thomas slowly stood and glanced at James, who nodded.

"The jury finds the defendant, Thomas J. Sampson, guilty of murder in the first degree, for the cold-blooded stabbing death of his wife, Evelyn Sampson. The jury recommends death by electrocution, for this cold-hearted murder. May this be a lesson to you, Thomas J. Sampson, and to all other murderers. That will be all."

Thomas felt his legs grow weak, and he slumped back into his chair. He looked helplessly at James.

"Sorry," was all he could say. "I really am sorry."

Thomas felt an arm slip into his as a police officer prepared to lead him away.

"We'll appeal this as soon as we can, Thomas," called James as the police took him away. "I promise!" Thomas thought he heard a quiver in James' voice, but didn't bother to look back. He felt tears forming in his own eyes.

He found his mother sitting near the back of the courtroom, bawling, with family and friends trying to console her. Thomas looked at the cops and then to his mother. "Make it quick," one of them said, leading Thomas over to his mother.

"I'm innocent, "he whispered to her. "I really am. I love Eve."

"I know, sugar. I know," was her answer. She hugged him for what might be the last time, and he was led away.

It was a long five months in jail. Death was constantly hanging over Thomas' head. As the time dragged on, it didn't become a question of if he would be put to death, but when. The daily visits by Thomas' mother and James were the only bright spots in Thomas' life.

The days dragged on and on, until one Friday, late in July. Thomas was meeting with James, but he knew something wasn't right in the way James was acting. Thomas finally asked what was wrong. "I can't keep it from you any longer," James started. "Our last appeal fell through today. It didn't work. I'm really sorry, Thomas," said James as Thomas buried his head in his hands and began to sob. "I really tried, I'm sorry," repeated James, placing a hand on Thomas' shoulder.

"I'm innocent! I didn't kill anyone! I've never killed anyone!" raved Thomas, sobbing harder and harder. Thomas' life was going to be taken for someone else, someone who would get off easily. It wasn't fair.

The execution chamber was a spotless as an operating room. Except here, they didn't save people. The chair sat in the middle of the room, with a door and a window on one side of the room. A small crowd was there to witness the execution—only Thomas' mother, Thomas' wife's parents, James, a priest, several police, a doctor, and the executioners. Thomas had his feet, hands, and chest strapped to the chair. Thomas prayed the telephone would ring, the governor on the other end, sparing his life. Thomas' heart was beating harder than ever in his life. The priest recited several prayers, gave him his last rights, and asked if he would like to say anything.

"I would like to forgive whoever murdered my wife. I hope she and her family know that I love her, and I hope they know I would never do anything as horrible as killing someone." Thomas turned to the priest, who stood, staring at him, his eyes beginning to water.

"A . . . Amen," he stuttered, turning to leave the chamber. The executioners squeezed a wet sponge over Thomas' head. They placed the head set on his head then walked to the corner. One switch, two switches, and the third. Thomas screamed his final scream as thousands of volts of electricity surged through his body. Blood poured from Thomas' mouth, like a red river, as he jerked like a rag doll. Thomas soiled his pants with urine, as his flesh burned from the heat of the electricity. The executioners cursed at the smell of burnt skin slowly filling the execution chamber. After

the corpse cooled down, the doctor listened to the heart of the victim. He looked up and nodded at the executioners. Thomas' life had ended.

It was a long few months after the execution. James tried to carry on his life as usual, but the memory of Thomas would not leave him. The blood, the scream, the whole moment stuck in his head. James was getting ready to leave his office late one Friday night. His secretary walked into his office and said, "There is someone here to see you, Mr. Coron."

"Send them in," he sighed, sitting down behind his oak desk. James was shocked to see Jennifer Walthrop walk into his office.

"Hello, sit down." She took a seat in front of his desk. "So?"

"I can't keep it in any longer," she whispered.

"What?" asked James, very confused.

"I've been keeping this a secret for a long time. I need to let it out." She took a deep breath and continued. "I was paid by the prosecutors to lie. I did see something the night of the murder."

James pulled a tape recorder out of his desk and motioned for her to continue.

"I saw exactly what Thomas explained. A man dressed in black ran out of Thomas' house and jumped into a car—no license plate—just as Thomas said. "That's all." She quickly got up and left, before he could react.

He sat there in confusion until his secretary brought in a new pile of mail and quickly left. His secretary had learned not to ask about his cases unless he involved her. He leafed through the mail until he came across a letter from the judicial system. He quickly opened the letter. He had to read it twice to make sure he read it right. One of the jurors had been found to be part of a white supremacy group. "So, racism had played a part," he thought to himself. It made sense; the all-white jury, the black defendant. Great time to find out—after the defendant was dead. This was too much for one day. The next day was not much less surprising, though.

James sat drinking his coffee and watching the morning news. A new flash said that an abandoned car had been found. The car had the same description that Thomas gave at his trial. James became more interested and turned the volume up on the TV. There also was a pair of gloves found in the car—covered with blood. The blood of Evelyn Sampson.

This was too much for James to take in all at once. His eyes filled with tears. Thomas had told the truth, but in this case, the truth wasn't good enough. Thomas had become the victim of a criminal justice system that is far from perfect. A system that tried to eliminate murder, but in trying to eliminate murder, became a murderer itself.

Appendix C

Sample Eighth-Grade Public Service Advertisement

HELLO? R U Listening? heLp!

I waNNa die.   LiFE suX.

JuSt caRe 4 me.

I maY not sHow iT, but I'm sCReaming inside... heLp me.

This could be YOUR friend screaming. Will you let them suffer? Help them get help. Now. Depression doesn't have to win, and you shouldn't let it.

Sponsored by TeenScene- Helping Teens Deal

Index

About the Authors

Chris Carlson is a former learning center director who has worked with teachers at the elementary, middle, and high school levels. She has participated in developing integrated units, writing district standards, teaching in-service classes, and setting building technology goals. She currently presents, writes, and consults on issues related to school libraries.

Ellen Brosnahan is a veteran middle school teacher who currently teaches an eighth grade literacy block at a middle school in suburban Chicago. Ellen has been a member of her district's language arts standards task force, and she frequently works on her district's curriculum development as a member of the curriculum council. Additionally, she often mentors new teachers and has facilitated several staff development courses for teachers on the teaching of writing and reading